From Outlaw to In-Law

From Outlaw to In-Law

How Multicultural Interfaith Couples Can Become Agents for Social Change

TANYA SADAGOPAN

Foreword by Duane Bidwell

WIPF & STOCK · Eugene, Oregon

FROM OUTLAW TO IN-LAW
How Multicultural Interfaith Couples Can Become Agents for Social Change

Copyright © 2024 Tanya Sadagopan. All rights reserved. Except for brief quotations in critical publications or reviews, no part of this book may be reproduced in any manner without prior written permission from the publisher. Write: Permissions, Wipf and Stock Publishers, 199 W. 8th Ave., Suite 3, Eugene, OR 97401.

Wipf & Stock
An Imprint of Wipf and Stock Publishers
199 W. 8th Ave., Suite 3
Eugene, OR 97401

www.wipfandstock.com

PAPERBACK ISBN: 978-1-6667-7950-9
HARDCOVER ISBN: 978-1-6667-7951-6
EBOOK ISBN: 978-1-6667-7952-3

11/21/24

Scripture quotations are taken from the New Revised Standard Version Updated Edition. Copyright © 2021 National Council of Churches of Christ in the United States of America. Used by permission. All rights reserved worldwide.

In loving memory of Jayanthi and Raghunathan Sadagopan
who despite cultural and religious traditions
loved me as their daughter.

Contents

Foreword by Duane Bidwell		ix
Acknowledgments		xi
An Introduction		xiii
1	When Love Leads to Justice	1
2	When We Feel Threatened	8
3	Disapproval and Conflict	13
4	Generational Conflict	18
5	Intersectionality	24
6	Dignity and Worth	31
7	Identity and Belonging	38
8	Expanding Identities and Double Belonging	46
9	Standing Up for Love	54
10	Remaking Rituals	61
11	The History of Us versus Them	65
12	Leaders for Change, Movements for Justice	83
13	Seeking Justice for Others	92
14	Reimagining Faith and God	98
15	Talking about Faith, Activism, and the Religious Other	106
16	Newfound Leadership Skills	116
17	Seeing Interfaith Leaders in Scripture	125
18	Love, Dignity, Equity, and Duty	134
19	Calling for Allies	141
20	Advice for Couples and Families	149

Contents

Appendix A: Photos of Multicultural Interfaith Couples   153

Appendix B: Qualitative Interview Summary Topics   157

Appendix C: Survey Questions on Interfaith Religious Engagement   159

Appendix D: Questions on Tension and Conflict   160

Appendix E: Questions on Social Change Agency   162

Appendix F: Eight Couples Selected for In-Depth Interviews   164

Glossary of Terms   166

Bibliography   171

Foreword

WHAT IT MEANS TO belong to one another stands at the heart of Tanya Sadagopan's life and ministry.

She writes from experience; for a quarter century, she and her husband Sriram have navigated the realities of multicultural interfaith marriage, raising two children to participate in both the Hindu and Christian traditions. A mother, professor, and United Church of Christ/Disciples of Christ pastor, Tanya trained as a sociologist (note that she's multiple even in her denominational commitment!). She brings a scholar's eye to her ministry and a pastor's heart to her scholarship, using both to craft this stellar text about couples bridging cultural and religious differences—and in the process creating positive social change beyond their kitchens and living rooms. The voices in the book, like Tanya's life, teach the value and practice of loving the "Other" despite anxiety, hesitation, and social pressure to reject unfamiliar people and behavior.

I have known Tanya for more than forty years. We met as undergraduates at Texas Christian University in Fort Worth, where a shared curiosity about world religions led us to explore Buddhist doctrines and practices, Lao devotional religion, and the meaning of values. Her questions led her to urban ministry in Chicago, where she directed a project on economic justice for the Seminary Consortium for Urban Pastoral Education, and to congregational ministry in rural and suburban areas of the Great Lakes. She pioneered both LGBTQIA+ outreach and advocacy and micro-grants for undocumented immigrant students.

Tanya and I reconnected during her doctoral work in Minnesota. At the time, I worked as a professor of spiritual care and counseling at Claremont School of Theology in California. I had just published the book *When One Religion Isn't Enough: The Lives of Spiritually Fluid People* (Beacon, 2018), and I knew that my colleagues in ministry needed Tanya's

Foreword

work. Religious leaders have few resources for engaging the realities of the multicultural interfaith families I had encountered in congregational and community life as a chaplain, spiritually integrative psychotherapist, and minister of the Presbyterian Church (USA). I encouraged Tanya to publish her research for an entirely selfish reason: I wanted to teach it to emerging pastors and chaplains.

The resulting book tackles three questions, one practical, one pastoral, and one theological. First, how do multicultural interfaith marriages and families become forces for good in their communities? This is the practical inquiry, and the book describes and interprets how participants in the study catalyze positive change in their extended families and neighborhoods. Second, how can congregations and religious communities best welcome multicultural interfaith families? This is the pastoral question, challenging religious leaders to become advocates for families that do not seem to "fit" in monoreligious, monocultural communities. The theological question might be most compelling: How do people move from exclusivist religion ("our way or the highway") and fear of the stranger to an inclusive embrace that recognizes multicultural interfaith families as gifts and not threats? In other words, how can each of us shift our values and commitments to create space for human and divine possibilities we have not imagined before?

Love is Tanya's answer to all three questions. Family and relational love, the love of one's child for the religious and cultural Other, and the Divine's love of diversity and multiplicity are, for her, the motivations and sources of change, welcome, and inclusivity.

I value *From Outlaw to In-Law* for many reasons. First, it features powerful narratives that illustrate what it takes to love, flourish, and lead across difference. Second, it teaches the power of curiosity to temper and transform fear. Third, it is a fantastic teaching resource for congregations and the academic classroom. But mostly, it is a witness to how compassion and advocacy contribute to the building of G-d's common/wealth, one family and home at a time.

The Rev. Duane Bidwell, PhD
Claremont, California

Acknowledgments

MY GRATITUDE EXTENDS TO the many people who have made this manuscript possible including my mentor, colleague, and friend Demian Wheeler; the United Theological Seminary of the Twin Cities where this research began during my doctorate of ministry; to Duane Bidwell who consistently encouraged me to make this work available to the public; to the members of First Congregational United Church of Christ of Janesville, Wisconsin, who provided me with continuing education time and a sabbatical that allowed me to expand this work; to Max Yeshaye Brumberg-Kraus, my personal editor, who read and challenged my work in ways that I had not considered; to Susan Katz Miller and the people of the Interfaith Families Project of Greater Washington, DC, Lisa Patriquin from The Guibord Center as part of their Inspiring Stories Project, and Kenneth Schoon from Westminster Presbyterian Church who each welcomed me and allowed me to present my work. My deepest love and appreciation is given to my husband of twenty-seven years, Sriram Sadagopan, and to our incredible multicultural interfaith children Nishanth and Nandini who are making their mark on the world and, in their own ways, are leaders for love and justice in their communities.

An Introduction

THIS BOOK BEGINS WITH love. The love for my husband across racial, cultural, and religious boundaries set the wheels in motion for this work. But it was the long and hard-won love of my mother-in-law that changed the direction of fifteen women and allowed them to get on a forbidden bus to attend her cremation where once only men were welcomed. We learned to love one another over time. I was not who she wanted for a daughter-in-law, yet we persevered through all the conflicts and challenges. What grew between us was a profound love. It changed both of our lives for the better. This book is about the transforming power that love has to change lives, remove prejudices, and open doors. It begins by standing up for the one you love, advocating for fair treatment, and finding allies along the way. When we stand up for uncommon love, advocate for equity, and find people who support that love, we may begin to see ways to support others facing similar challenges in other areas of our lives. This is justice work. The steps we have taken on the path of love seeking justice is not unique to my family. I designed a survey that was shared around the world, couple to couple, which allowed me to arrange interviews and meet with eight remarkable multicultural interfaith couples. These couples' stories speak to how they each grew in their ability to advocate for the ones they loved and how their relationships lead them to new opportunities for justice work in their communities. The journey of my husband and myself is mirrored in their lives. These couples' religious traditions span Hinduism, Christianity, Islam, Sikhism, Atheism, Buddhism, Catholicism, and Unitarian Universalism, daring to love across cultures that divide us.

  This book draws on the work of pluralist theologians such as Margorie Suchocki and Paul Knitter whose contributions support an understanding of how to better relate to and appreciate distinct religious perspectives from people of different religious traditions than one's own. For example, while

An Introduction

one may appreciate other traditions and desire to engage in mutual dialogue and service together, which would represent a pluralist understanding of other religions, others may desire to engage with the religiously othered only so far as they are able to see their own traditional values and beliefs reflected in them, which would represent an inclusivist understanding of other religions. Finally, someone may feel it is their religious duty to either exclude or convert one who is from another religious tradition, which would suggest their theology comes out of an exclusivist understanding of other religious traditions. We will meet couples who desire to take their beliefs and theologies and put them into action. This reflects commitments echoed in Helen Slessarev Jamir and Walter Brueggemann's works that speak of *the prophetic tradition* and where our faiths call us to move toward acts that bring freedom, access, and equality to all. These are ideas of liberation. Theologians that espouse liberation such as feminist, womanist, and non-Western theologians remind us to examine our own religious, cultural, and gender positions of relative power and privilege. At the very least, while we hear these stories from multicultural interfaith couples from around the world, my hope is that we will work to decenter white-Christian-male experiences as the vantage point from whence we judge relationships and understand their relative acceptance or exclusion in their communities. My desire is to point to the complex contexts each couple dwells within that cross religious, cultural, race, caste, national, as well as gender differences. My goal is to lift up stories and engage with people who are authoring their own theologies of religions from within their multicultural interfaith contexts in a variety of national locations. Theirs are practical theologies that come from interfaith experiences that often inspire adaptation and social change. This contextual work is not easy. In their stories you will see my preference toward couples who value equity in their relationships and tend to share cultural and religious traditions with one another. My own multicultural interfaith journey with my husband of twenty-seven years will be found in personal stories and reflections in many of the chapters. The names of the couples reflect the requests of the couples I interviewed. Some are pseudonyms, which they have chosen for themselves; others are their actual names. I have not indicated which names belong to which categories.

Much of the research material and some of the stories found in this book were first published in my 2021 doctoral dissertation, "Faith, Fault Lines, and Family: A Study of Multicultural, Interfaith Couples and Social Change Agency," under the direction of Dr. Demian Wheeler at United

An Introduction

Theological Seminary of the Twin Cities. This book is entirely reorganized from that original work, adapted for a broader audience, and additional material and stories have been added, including one additional couple interview. The chapters of this book are organized around experiences that are common to multicultural interfaith couples; for instance, you will read about topics concerning when we feel threatened, when we face disapproval and conflict, when we stand up for love and reimagine our faith and who God is in our lives, to name just a few. While the chapters are intended to build upon one another, they can be read out of sequence based on where the reader's interest takes them.

This body of work integrates my training as both a sociologist and a public theologian. The intersecting aspects of culture, faith, social movements, and social change have been the lenses through which I view my world. When people form deep spiritual connections with those who come from distinct social, racial, cultural, economic, or religious backgrounds it sparks within me joy, inspiration, and innovation. I believe it mirrors the imagination of God. When a relationship of this kind is formed between two people—call them "couples"—I believe they are called to be a part of the noble task of making the world a better place. When couples marry across great oceans of differences, the Holy One invites them to be cocreators in increasing love and justice, equity and dignity. Thus, from my vantage point, multicultural interfaith couples have an opportunity to participate in a holy endeavor that has the possibility of uniting the human family across nationality, race, caste, culture, language, sexuality, gender, ability, and age. I align myself with those who share these goals and commitments—some are pluralist theologians of religions, while others are liberation, womanist, ecofeminist, and queer theologians.

My experience of God is most clearly felt in the transformative experiences of uncommon love across differences. These relationships may happen when forgiveness without merit occurs; acceptance and dignity is freely given where shame and despair once lived; and when people experience something sacred and holy together who are from cultures that bridge chasms of fear and hostility. I see the world through the lens of the four transforming ideas of love, dignity, equity, and duty—the absence of which causes great pain, the presence of which brings great joy.

This book is written for people who love someone whom their family forbids. I hope within these pages you will find stories of others who have loved the outlaw and, over time, found a way to reconcile conflicts between their exceptionally different families. This book is written for parents who have discovered that their adult child(ren) wanted to marry someone outside of their religious community as well as racial, ethnic, or cultural expectations. May this book help them see that these differences between their family and their children's chosen partners can be a blessing. This book is written for professionals in the academy or in counseling to give access to research and stories of multicultural interfaith couples from a variety of religious traditions. May this book help illustrate the ways that intersectionality can enhance religious expression and identity formation.

And finally, this book is written for clergy and religious professionals. As a clergyperson myself, I know we have power to exclude and shun or welcome and approve people who choose to marry someone outside of our religious traditions. Their desire to marry across religions may pose a conflict within you, as a clergyperson, between upholding the traditions of your faith and your desire to provide a loving and welcoming community where faithful people can grow in their religious practice. May this book give you examples of successful couples who helped their families grow because they married outside of their religious tradition and, subsequently, their individual faith was deepened. Clergy have the power to bless and mentor couples. Religious leaders also have the power to change the systems and rules surrounding marriage that prevent welcoming multicultural interfaith families fully into our faith communities.

May this book, *From Outlaw to In-Law*, lead us all towards more loving and inclusive communities, especially for those who love the person they were raised to condemn, fear, or despise.

I

When Love Leads to Justice

STANDING JUST OUTSIDE THE gate of the complex of newly constructed buildings in a suburb of Chennai, India, I did not notice the women who had gathered around me clad in colorful sarees like mine. We were all grieving the death of my *amma*. My co-sister and I had just completed the preparations of her body inside of the small living room of the flat she and her husband had built a few years prior. We poured vessels of water over her body and then dressed her in the last saree she would wear as she would be sent into the holy fires of cremation. As her daughters-in-law it was our duty to ready her physical remains to be taken to the crematorium. The final Hindu religious rites were to be performed there. Standing on the road just beside the bus that would carry the mourners, I began to cry. *Appa* instructed me, "You cannot go. Women are not allowed." Bereaved and shocked, I begged, "Please *Appa*, let me on the bus. I loved her. She loved me. Please let me go to the cremation." Tears streaming down my face, my pleading continued, "She was a mother to me. Please *Appa*, I loved her too."

Earlier my co-sister had bathed *Amma* with the smaller of two vessels we filled with water. She had known *Amma* one year; such a short time. My vessel, a curved traditional *kalish*, was much larger and took longer to fill in their tiny kitchen. Ten years together changed both of us. The water slowly filling the *kalish* seemed to know the fullness of those years as it rose to kiss the brim. My co-sister, who was my husband's younger brother's wife, approached *Appa* and said, "In my family, the women are allowed to go to the cremation sites." This is significant because my co-sister is Iyengar, and I am not. I am a white midwestern Christian woman from a poor family of Ohio farmers and Alabama ministers. While I am the eldest daughter-in-law in this Hindu extended family and have special privileges and responsibilities, I can be easily dismissed as an outsider when it comes to religious rituals. I straddle the two worlds of being a cherished family member and an unwelcome outsider. This is the nature of belonging and not belonging at the same time. I am a white Christian woman in a brown Hindu man's world. My husband and I are as different as toast is to *dosai*. Yet we belong together like toast belongs in a toaster and *dosai* belongs on the *tawa*: both can live in the same kitchen. Ours is a multicultural, international, interfaith marriage.

There are no other Hindu Iyengar religious rituals that are more sacred or more important than the Hindu rituals conducted at the time of death. Our Indian Hindu family has strong patriarchal views that require adherence to religious orthodoxy. At that moment, I was not thinking about what was right or wrong. I loved my *amma* and wanted to be with her to the end. My co-sister's father approached *Appa* and, together with the other men, began arguing about the legitimacy of my claim to come on the bus. *Appa* was a well-respected man in the family and religious community. He looked at me and then to my husband and said to him, "She can come." Hands folded in prayer bowing to him, I thanked him and turned to board the bus. Wiping my eyes, I walked down the aisle and sat down. As I did, only then did I notice behind me were fifteen other women, who got on the bus after me. *Amma*'s sisters, co-sisters, and her close friends all took their seats to join me and the men on *Amma*'s final journey.

This surprised me. It was not just a matter of *love for me*, this was a matter *of justice* for *the rest of the women* in the family. In this orthodox South Indian Hindu family, women customarily were not permitted to attend cremation ceremonies. *Amma* had four sisters and six co-sisters and other intimate friends, whom she treated like sisters. The cultural barrier barring these women from attending was lifted that day in part because of my own advocacy to attend my *amma*'s cremation. Justice was a matter of love. I did not intend to challenge or change cultural norms in that moment; I simply felt it was the *right thing to do*. As a result of these actions born out of love, other women, who loved her deeply, benefited and one avenue toward equality was opened for the women of my family.

My ministry as a leader for social change in the United States has been fraught with challenges of belonging and constrained by issues of religious orthodoxy. My husband is a South Indian Tamil Iyengar Brahmin Hindu. He and I have differences that span race, religion, culture, language, and national origin. Tamil is the language he speaks; Iyengar refers to the particular *Vaishnavite* Brahmin caste his family belongs to; Hindu is his religion; South Indian refers to his culture and race as well as the region from which he comes; and India is his nationality. Our marriage demonstrates the blessings that intersectional relationships can bring. It is at the intersection of our multiple identities that bring both challenges and blessings to our families and community. Yet traditional family values from both sides of our families did not make the start of our life together easy. The cultural wars between the "East and the West," Hindu and Christians, and white women and brown men were about to erupt in the communities that surrounded us. The world was sure we did not belong together.

Our interfaith marriage complicated my choice to go into ministry. Others, who had the power and authority to approve or disapprove of my ordination into Christian ministry, questioned the legitimacy of my call to the profession. Together my husband and I have enjoyed twenty-seven fruitful years of marriage sharing in each other's faith traditions and rituals while raising our children in both religious traditions—Hinduism and Christianity. This is still considered to be a problem in most religious circles—*you cannot be both Christian and Hindu.* You are expected to choose one and deny the other. It is still a widely held practice within religious institutions that have standards for ordination of clergy that a person cannot hold two religious identities at once and remain *orthodox* in their beliefs. Does a Christian married to a Hindu belong in the role of leadership as our Christian minister? Does a Jewish person married to a Christian belong in the leadership as our rabbi? When committees responsible for my ordination considered my calling to ministry, I heard comments such as "if she cannot convert her own husband to Christianity, how can she be a good minister?" These are matters not only of religious practice but also questions regarding leadership. Clergy must look the part, act the part, and adhere to traditional standards of who belongs in these roles, because they must maintain the purity of the faith. Welcoming clergy spouses from other religious traditions outside the faith, especially if they are from traditions not tied to their own religious history, is considered hypocritical at best and apostasy at worst. In this regard, justice and hospitality do not matter when it comes to training and ordaining our leaders for service in our congregations. While faith traditions may seem open to the view of other religious traditions, inherent prejudices against interfaith marriages sit on the committees who have the power to decide who is and who is not ordained.

For all these years, balancing my family life and my ministry required walking the line between my public professional life with my private multicultural interfaith married life. I could not share openly about our interfaith family without raising questions about the orthodoxy of my Christianity and my ability to be an effective Christian leader. Yet, it is my marriage to my Hindu husband that has deepened my understanding of Christian Scripture, provided a more practical approach to religious rituals, and created for me a more meaningful faith. These are desirable leadership qualities.

Interfaith dialogue in my case was not academic but real exchanges between people who love each other and disagree about a whole range of topics. Ours is an interfaith, cross-cultural, interracial, and cross-class marriage. He was the richer, more educated, more stable of the two of us. My family was among the white working poor in Florida. Divorce, alcoholism, violence, and poverty all plagued my youth. Always fighting to be heard and struggling to belong in my own conservative Christian family, ironically, it was within an orthodox Indian Hindu family where I found my belonging. I am among the first generation in my family to graduate from high school as well as college. Education is where I found my liberation. I worked hard to be accepted within my husband's family. I was not who they had in mind for an arranged marriage with their fair-skinned, American-educated PhD, firstborn son. Soon, I was not just their daughter-in-law, I was their *daughter*, whom they showered with gold and jewels, love and tenderness. Yet arguments and mutual frustrations grew as our cultures and ideas clashed and reoriented around conversations of rules and religions, patriarchy and privilege. By living with and caring for his parents, I have engaged in some sort of interfaith dialogue for the last twenty-seven years. At times conversing and converging, conflicting and correcting one another, each of us have grown in remarkable ways. All of us have been transformed by the experience of having been a part of a multicultural interfaith multigenerational family.

Living at the intersection between these two very different communities has given me insight into the complexities surrounding families who share more than one religious tradition and hold more than one cultural identity. Experiencing a lifetime of cultural tensions and resolving religious conflicts have allowed me to develop skills that have made me a better *Christian* leader. Our passionate conversations about God, theology, gratitude, prayer, compassion, suffering, birth, death, and activism across our two religious traditions while drinking our morning *chai* together has undoubtably made me a better Christian and made my husband a more faithful practitioner of Hinduism as well.

You may know a family like mine. You may be considering marrying across cultural and religious differences. You may be striving to teach the complexity of interreligious relationships or desire to show how interfaith relationships within families are about more than just interfaith dialogue. I want you to know that you are not alone in your questions. Multicultural interfaith couples lead complex lives. The family dynamics and religious conflicts these couples encounter are as varied as the world we live in. The wars abroad come home and complicate the love they share. Families that deal with adult children who marry an outsider know that hurt, fear, and pain run deep. Emotions run high. People say and do things that offend and may cause irreparable harm. But there is hope. Where there is love, there is hope for a future that one could not imagine. It is because of this love that couples will forgive the hurt, teach acceptance, model kindness, and, in the process, learn together and grow closer. Because of love, parents will forgive and be patient to learn why their child could possibly love someone whom their community taught them to condemn. These remarkable people have learned to navigate and understand the complex family and community relationships that make up their everyday life. I believe that people who marry across religious traditions, race, culture, and nationality can be agents for positive change in our hometowns. Perhaps these are the kinds of leaders we need to help us navigate the rugged terrain of this era, which is fraught with war, religious extremism, political polarization, and racial disparities.

Multicultural interfaith couples face multiple forms of discrimination because of their intersectional identities. Our family faced a variety of challenges, including navigating the complex immigration system in the United States. For us, issues of immigration were not academic conversations or mere news events. These policies impact the lives of real people. It was my responsibility to shepherd my father-in-law to all his required citizenship meetings, a process that took over five years. I did the same for his son, my husband, twenty years prior. Another challenge is that high holy days for Hindus, Jews, and Muslims are not honored by school calendars based in the Christian paradigm. Grief is limited to three days off within most American workplace cultures. Yet, for Hindu rites to be performed for one's parents requires a minimum of fourteen days off, not including travel days.

Having enough funeral leave for international workers is not a theoretical argument, it is a matter of justice. Three days of funeral leave that is offered in the United States is entirely insufficient. It took us more than sixteen days to complete the rituals and travel halfway across the world to India from Chicago. Each day was filled with mandatory religious rites to be performed. The formalities of the business side of death cannot begin until those rituals are completed.

Language becomes a cultural barrier as well. There is no equivalent to a "co-sister" in my white American Christian cultural understanding. She is not a relative. She is my sister in marriage. The intimacy of that relationship is conveyed in the language. For instance, it feels wrong to say "in-laws," which is an English phrase. For me, my in-laws will always be my *appa* and *amma*, that is, my Indian dad and mom. Evidenced by their love and care for me, they made it clear that I was their adopted daughter. I have lived in both worlds, Indian and American, as well as Hindu and Christian. I have experienced prejudice and discrimination based on the color of my skin in India, witnessed the challenges that two sets of religious holidays for our kids posed for them by their schools in the Chicago suburbs, and I felt the judgmental eyes upon us in churches and temples at home and abroad. We did not seem to belong anywhere. In the process I have learned to navigate all these different worlds and learned the complexity surrounding the differences between our cultures, races, religions, and nationalities. I have learned the importance of standing up for love and advocating for justice for my family. Therefore, standing up and advocating on behalf of those who are also outsiders is easier for me because of the experiences within my own multicultural interfaith family.

Perhaps mine is not a unique experience. What if multicultural interfaith couples around the world are unsuspecting leaders for social change in their communities? Is it not possible that they could become potential agents for positive change because of their ability to navigate complex multicultural interreligious issues? My research suggests that *sustained long-term interfaith dialogue within multicultural interfaith couples contributes to their capacity to become positive agents of social change within their communities*. And if multicultural interfaith couples are a source for social change in their communities, how might clergy and other leaders within faith communities better support and utilize the gifts they bring in our communities? Asked another way, are multicultural interfaith couples an untapped source for nuanced leadership?

My research is based on in-depth personal qualitative interviews with eight multicultural interfaith couples spanning nine religious affiliations and five different countries. These interviews explored the practical lived experiences of multicultural interfaith couples who engaged in sustained conversations about God and practiced their faith over the life of their marriages. I developed a new survey tool to measure three distinct concepts. I wanted to understand the types of religious activities the couple engaged in with one another. I refer to this as interfaith religious engagement. Secondly, I developed survey questions that looked at measuring tension and conflict the couple experienced. The ways their family was supportive or not, when there were requests for conversion to their partner's religious tradition, and if there were instances of discrimination or prejudicial comments gave me an indication of the amount of conflict a couple experienced in their community. Thirdly, survey questions centered around the type and number of volunteer and social justice activities the couples engaged in, which measured the level of their social change agency.

The demographics of the survey respondents was remarkable. Fifty-six couples from ten different religious traditions, nineteen states in the United States, and ten countries around the world responded to this unique survey. Seven of these couples were selected for in-depth intimate interviews. An additional eighth couple was interviewed in 2024. The interviews explored the challenges the couples faced during the formation of their relationship and discussed ways in which the couples exhibited social change agency within their communities. Marriage in this case created immersive multicultural interfaith experiences and provided these couples with a repertoire of skills that are useful for navigating conflict. These skills developed and were refined when clashes of culture, race, gender, or faith resulted in instances of inequity, discrimination, or injustice. They found themselves with a new sense of identity given by their multicultural interfaith marital status. By advocating for the one they love within the communities that would traditionally exclude their partner, they learned how to advocate for others who are also discriminated against. These couples teach us how deep love for their partner leads them towards the work of justice for others who face injustice in their communities.

2

When We Feel Threatened

When a young man who is Muslim brings home a prospective bride who is Sikh, there is caution and hesitancy even before the planned encounter with his parents takes place. The stakes are high, and their parents' cultural memories are long. Within the Indian subcontinent there is a long-standing conflict between these two religious traditions that originates with the invasion of the Indian subcontinent by Muslims. The conflict between these two cultures and religions continued for many centuries as Mughal rulers persecuted Sikhs for generations.[1] Animosity remains within the hearts of both family's traditions from the on-again off-again conflicts between the cultures and religious traditions. When our Muslim groom brings home his Sikh bride to his parents, the family conflict is not only personal; it is also cultural, religious, and geopolitical. The bride-to-be is instantly perceived as a threat to that family's way of life. To appreciate the tension and conflict that these couples endure, and their ability to effect change within their families and communities, we must see them in a larger cultural and national context.

One young couple can help us understand this dynamic: his family is Muslim, her family comes from another religious tradition that originated in India called Sikhism. Kamran and Kamalpreet faced stereotypes and prejudicial comments from both of their families once they revealed their relationship to their parents. While they were engaged just a few days prior to our interview, they have been together for eight years. Stories of entrapment of Sikh girls by Muslim men are used to question the

---

1. See for instance "18th and 19th Centuries" in the bibliography.

legitimacy of their relationship as well as to question the motivation of Kamran toward Kamalpreet's Sikh faith. "My family was really focused on these Muslim men getting these girls to fall in love with them and then converting them and then like just leaving them, really isolating them and, you know, breaking those family ties so that they become dependent on the man. So, my parents were like, 'Well, is he like that?'" The animosity between the religious traditions runs deep and is based on generations of violence beginning with the Moghul period in India's history. Talking about her own faith tradition, Kamalpreet continues, "There are stories where the Sikh gurus were buried alive and soldiers and everything were buried alive in cement by Muslims. I had to hear tons of stuff like that." Kamran was very understanding of these prejudicial statements and fears coming from Kamalpreet's family. He is a history buff, exploring the heritage of his family as well as religious conflicts across the generations. While his father, who is agnostic, was supportive, his mother, who is a practicing Muslim, was not. "My mom, she's a very practicing Muslim. She wears the headscarf; she prays five times a day. When she found out, she was just not accepting of it. She was basically saying it's her duty as my mom to make sure I marry a Muslim and that our bloodlines continue to be Muslim." His mother still identifies with being Pakistani and has some family who still reside there. Kamran does not identify as Pakistani but honors his mother's history and heritage and appreciates her reluctance to accept his relationship with Kamalpreet. Speaking sensitively about his mother, Kamran shares, "My mom was very concerned about what she would tell her family overseas. Pakistan is a religious republic. They don't have this cultural concept of religious freedom for the people. If you're not a Muslim, the impacts in your life will be very far [reaching] and you might be more subject to violence or hate. So, the idea of even having friends that are not Muslim in Pakistan is probably very rare." It has taken his mother many years to come to accept their relationship, but she has. Both families now support their relationship.

THE STRANGER

When couples who love across religious, cultural, and national boundaries encounter resistance at home, they are often dealing with the challenge of whether their family will *welcome this stranger into their family*. Their faith is strange; their culture is strange; their country of origin is strange; their language and food preferences may also be strange. When we feel threatened, it is normal to want to protect our family, our culture, our religious beliefs, and the way we live. Before we get to know them, people outside of our traditions threaten our sense of safety because we are responding to conflicts embedded in the geopolitical landscapes of our lives. Strangers can be threatening. The national experience of a crisis at our borders reflects the crisis of identities we are experiencing within the local communities where we live. How we feel and respond to welcoming *this stranger* our adult child wants to marry is a local manifestation of a global phenomenon. Why is there often such a strong response to *the stranger*?

One answer lies in globalization. Eleazar Fernandez, in his book *Burning Center, Porous Borders: The Church in a Globalized World*, speaks of the rise of conflicts and terrorism and ties it to the spread of Western Civilization. "Predatory corporate globalization is a major triggering factor in many expressions of terrorism around the world. Globalization, as a shorthand term that represents not only the economy but also the spread of the Western project (civilization, liberal democracy, and secularism), has surfaced in many fundamentalist militants' rhetoric as a threat that must be stopped by all means and at all costs."[2] Let that phrase, "it must be stopped at all costs," echo in your ears. That desire to stop *it*—the infiltration of other cultures into my community—at all costs is compounding the efforts of children's ability to share the love and intimacy they feel with their chosen partner. In the process of economic globalization, as people move around the world so do our religious practices. Faith then has also become globalized. When the one we love comes from next door but is a world away from our own family, we may experience a crisis of our own identity. When this happens, how will we respond?

What might you do when you feel threatened by someone who is new to you? What if you bump into them in a grocery store? What if they move next door? What if they want to marry your daughter? They dress differently, eat differently, speak differently, and look differently than you and your family. Do you feel curious or are you fearful? The two primary human responses to when we feel threatened by the stranger are to isolate and protect ourselves or to be curious and learn more about them. The parents of young Kamran and Kamalpreet want to protect their children and so they work to prevent their relationship from going further. Kamran and Kamalpreet are compassionate because they know the histories of trauma on both sides of their families. They are patient and help their parents move

---

2. Fernandez, *Burning Center, Porous Borders*, 14–15.

from fear to curiosity about their relationship. But that takes time and a willingness to listen to those deeper fears that come from living through traumatic experiences during cultural conflict, war, and displacement. Generations of pain cannot be overcome in a few months.

Fernandez suggests that we can reclaim a theology of *welcoming the stranger* from Jewish and Christian traditions, especially as a way of countering the adverse effects that the export of colonial Christianity has had on diaspora churches. He writes, "the stranger is the classic Other, which is also a classic metaphor for the presence of the Divine."[3] If encountering the stranger is actually an encounter with the divine, then our approach may shift from one of fear and conflict to one of hospitality and welcome. Within my Hindu family's tradition of hospitality toward the stranger, there is an essential skill that is at the heart of the faith. When a new bride enters the house, she is greeted as if she is the embodiment of *Laxmi*, the goddess of wealth and prosperity. She is greeted as a divine guest, given flowers, a choice meal, and the finest gifts. It is believed that this new bride can bring favor on the house or its downfall. As a bride who enters the house, she is aware of this religious metaphor and takes seriously the responsibility to be a blessing to this family. The threat of her strange presence is mitigated by a mutual commitment to extend welcome and be a blessing. This is one of the rituals that has been practiced in arranged marriages in Hindu households for generations. But what happens when adult children want to arrange their own marriages?

Colleen and Shiva are a UU-Buddhist/Hindu couple. They faced a great deal of resistance and conflict when their relationship was forming. Shiva's parents expected to arrange his marriage to a nice, educated Tamil girl. That did not happen. Shiva's parents are Iyer Brahmins from South India and are religiously orthodox. When making important decisions, especially with regards to marriage partners for their children, they will seek advice from their family astrologer. Shiva describes sharing the news with his parents, "[I said to my parents,] this is what I am choosing for myself. That was very hard for them to get. [They said], '*Why would you do this to us?*'" Shiva's choice to marry Colleen was an act against his parents. This unorthodox match would bring prying questions, shame, and ridicule to the family from others in their extended family, their religious community, and neighborhood. This relationship was bad news for Shiva's parents and their standing in the community.

---

3. Fernandez, *Burning Center, Porous Borders*, 224.

Adherence to the practice of arranging marriages is a method of cultural preservation. The desire to hold on to purity of that culture grows stronger the more religiously adherent the family of origin is, the higher the caste, and the part of India where the family lives. South India tends to be more religiously conservative than North India. Religious rules and traditional practices may be more relaxed in some North Indian families than in the South. In an effort to stop this marriage, Shiva's parents sought support not only from family who belonged to their religious Iyer community but also from their Sai Baba ashram. Their strong objection to this match with Colleen is in part related to the cultural conservatism of Shiva's family of origin.

Shiva's parents held the view that Colleen had placed some kind of an evil spell on Shiva. It makes sense that they needed to engage religious rituals to undo this negative influence that she had over him. Shiva describes their desperation to prevent this disaster in the life of their son. "Is there a way out of it for [my parents]; can they go and do some rituals and he would be free of this demon? There's this word '*parigharam*,' which means you can do something to move the evil energies out. The word in Tamil means, if I do these things for you God, please clear these obstacles. Go to specific temples, a lot of *poojas* and *homams* based on what the astrologers told them would be necessary to get over the bad period." *Poojas* are prayer rituals often conducted in the home. *Homams* are religious rituals that involve sacred Sanskrit chanting, which require a priest to be present. These are performed in front of the sacred fire known as *Agni*—the fire is the holy witness, a symbol of God's presence in the room. Shiva's parents sought advice from their astrologer, who prescribed prayer rituals to be performed at certain times—like a prescription given to combat a particular illness. If the rituals were to have the desired effect, it would result in the ending of his relationship with Colleen. All these rituals were conducted in an effort to release the evil influence over Shiva that was causing him to want to marry this woman. Colleen was a threat to their way of life. They were not curious about her nor interested in why their son loved this stranger in their midst. In a very real way, they believed their son was under her spell.

3

Disapproval and Conflict

IN OCTOBER OF 1996 I was sitting on the little twin bed in my boyfriend's college basement apartment in Ohio. Making an international call to India was expensive, often costing over one dollar per minute, so he used a paid international calling service called Reliance that required ten digits of pre-dialing before beginning to enter the country code and local phone number of his parents. His parents were themselves part of a South Indian Orthodox Hindu Iyengar Brahmin family. This was no ordinary call—this was *the call* when he was going to tell *them about us.* The international ring tone gave way to his father's voice, and he began to speak in a language I did not understand—his native tongue of Tamil. Soon the conversation became heated, and his father's voice and tone raised. Peppered with occasional English words here and there, I could make out that the conversation was not going well. What was a hopeful afternoon turned into a fearful and conflictual period for my boyfriend as well as our relationship. They would not accept a white American Christian woman as a daughter-in-law. They would gladly arrange a Hindu match for him with a suitable girl if he would come home over the holidays. This situation, often the content of my nightmares, could not happen. My fear grew out of the experience of my dear friend Karel,[1] who had fallen in love with a Tamil Brahmin man. He went home on his own without her to convince his parents of his relationship with Karel. When he returned, he broke off his engagement with her by sharing that in India he had gotten married to a new Indian Hindu Brahmin bride he had just met. Karel was devastated. The pressure to marry

1. A pseudonym.

within one's religion, caste, and culture is very high. People may choose to stay within their religious and cultural traditions rather than deal with the fallout from defying their parents' expectations. This is how the tensions between our two families began—conflicting values, different religions, separate cultures, and distinct nations began to clash in our young lives. It was unlikely our relationship would survive these conflicts.

We live in a global economy driven by a variety of industries and demands for talent and labor. Access to university education and advanced training along with market demands have encouraged immigration worldwide. The United States is often a driver and recipient of those immigration trends. As people from a variety of backgrounds and cultures come together in communities and workplace environments, they build relationships outside of their culture of origin and religious traditions. Love happens. Relationships develop. Sparks fly. And suddenly religious conflicts and culture wars flare up around the dinner table, in the temple, and over the phone on international calls home. These were tense times.

Cultural wars are the content of the daily news. Multicultural interfaith couples face a variety of conflicts and understand the impact of those cultural wars on their daily lives. Yet how can we measure the tensions and conflicts couples' experiences in their relationship? Living with tension and working through conflicts across so many differences might provide insight into how to navigate complex global environments. I wanted to find a way to measure that conflict in my research. The ways in which I attempted to measure the level of tension and conflict a couple experienced in the multicultural interfaith relationship primarily centered around three factors: (1) the acceptance of their relationship by their respective families; (2) instances of prejudice or discrimination they experienced in their couple; and (3) suggestions or direct requests that they or their partner convert to the other religious tradition by their future in-laws. Tension and conflict were a factor in many of these couples' lives. While one-third of these couples reported often experiencing instances of prejudice or discrimination, nearly 75 percent of those surveyed were able to list specific details of instances where they or their partner had experienced discrimination or prejudice based on religious affiliation, racial background, caste, cultural, or ethnic identity. Many incidents listed were experienced while they were together. Some were prevented from entering a temple with their partner without explicitly signing a document of belief. Others experienced hostility at marrying outside of their faith tradition. Prejudicial comments included, "he will lock you in the cellar," seeing scared looks on people's faces, changing in tone of people's voices, or being told they were "dating the enemy." One respondent wrote that her boss called her into his office to discuss "her choice of boyfriend." From direct housing discrimination to being pulled over by the police, the discriminatory acts were varied and impacted where they lived, their work environment, and their ability to freely eat or shop in local establishments.

Early on in these relationships, some of those couples surveyed had either their parents or their partner's family suggest or directly ask them to convert to their partner's religious tradition. This represented 24 percent of our couples who experienced direct or indirect requests to leave their own religious tradition and convert to their partner's tradition. When one person is asked to convert to their partner's religion it immediately suggests that there is something wrong with their own religious tradition and they do not belong unless they convert. This is a highly stressful occurrence in the life of a young couple and adds a great deal of tension to the formation of the interfaith relationship. And yet there is hope. It is possible that the relationship between the religious outsider, the *outlaw*, and their future *in-law* can change for the better over time. Many of our couples saw a big change in their families support of their relationship, reporting that over 50 percent experienced their families growing to accept and support their relationship over time. Yet, over time 5 percent experienced their families becoming less supportive and viewing their relationship more negatively. Some conflicts can become engrained, and the chasm between families deepen. While these scenarios are fewer, the reality of the relationship can and does put such a strain on the blended families that adult children may be cut off from their parents because of who they chose to marry. This could be initiated on either side, by uncompromising adult children or by their unaccepting parents. A small percentage, 3 percent, had little to no contact with the other side of their family, and 14 percent continued to have unsupportive family members. One wonders how these multicultural interfaith couples may have grown if their respective families were more supportive and had regular contact with their adult children. If there is to be growth, both the young interfaith couple and the elder parents must be willing to stay in communication when it is difficult and learn to trust their love for one another. I believe that, ultimately, it is because of love that we will forgive, try again, and be willing to learn new things about the uncompromising and unaccepting family in our lives. By working across differences that would normally cause sustained conflict and discriminatory acts, each member of the extended family will learn nuanced skills of peacemaking and conflict resolution that they did not have prior.

Adam and Maria, a Jewish/Catholic couple, faced significant discrimination in the beginning of their relationship. Adam and Maria have been married for two years and live in a lower-level flat in Costa Rica with their eighteen-month-old son. Above them live Maria's parents.

We spoke with one another using a video conference platform. Their parents, grandparents, and child moved between the upstairs and downstairs units freely throughout our interview time together. Maria understands English but speaks more freely in Spanish. Adam, who is fluent in Spanish and English, translated for her during our time together. Later I would pay a translator to have Maria's words transcribed and translated directly. Maria's quotes are in her own words but are translated from the original Spanish. They live in what we refer to in India as a *joint family*, with three generations living together. Early in their relationship, they both faced cultural and religious stereotypes about their chosen partner as well as institutional discrimination. Adam is Jewish and Maria is Catholic. Initially they were not sure if they should even date. Maria explains, "The important part about these differences of culture and religion came out in this moment when we were deciding whether to date or not, given all the challenges with the distance, culture, and religion. Adam wasn't sure how I or my family felt about Jews, because in Costa Rica there aren't many Jews. Very few." Costa Rica is a Central American country south of Nicaragua and north of Panama filled with rainforests and mountains. It is one of a few countries in the world that established Roman Catholicism as the official state religion, with 57 percent of the population identifying as Roman Catholic.[2] Adam shares what it is like to live in a small Catholic town in Costa Rica, "We still encounter ignorance here, just because in this town, I might be one of the only Jews. And so, we still encounter people who just out of ignorance say comments." Adam, from the United States, is often the first non-Catholic person people in the community meet. He comes from a culturally Jewish family who is less religious. Adam's grandfather survived Nazi Germany and fought in World War II. In Maria's community there are both curiosity as well as misconceptions that conflate Judaism with Islamic traditions. "Well, I was told that Jews have multiple wives. They confuse the Jews with Arab religions a lot, like what they see in movies. One time I

---

2. Wikipedia, "Costa Rica."

told a client of mine that I was going to get married to a Jew, and she said [gasps] 'How scary!'" When Adam shared the news that he was marrying someone who is Catholic with his friends, they would ask, "So you guys, does that mean you're going to have eight children?" Much of their young relationship has been one of exposing and correcting misconceptions and stereotypes about one another's religious traditions with their families, friends, and community.

Shiva and Colleen experienced disapproval from both sides of their families. Shiva's parents, who are Orthodox Hindu Iyer Brahmins, were in shock and disbelief when he announced his engagement to Colleen. When Shiva talked to his parents, "This came as a total shock to them that this was happening, so they were trying to find any kind of reason. It can't be our son. It has to be something else." They refused to offer their blessing for the marriage, were extremely reluctant to meet Colleen even when she traveled to India, and they hid their son's relationship from their community. They were ashamed and worried what their community would think of them given he was planning to marry outside of their religion, culture, and homeland. They did not just express their disapproval; they went to great lengths to save their son from this woman.

4

Generational Conflict

CONFLICT IS COMMON IN extended families. We may disagree about what we value, how to raise our kids, what teams we root for, or which political candidates we favor. What is less common in marriages between partners who are from the same country, culture, race, and religion is when that conflict stems from generations of displacement, war, and political upheaval. When families survive cultural displacement, their traditional ways of life are left behind in the homelands they were forced to leave. Those of us who receive the resettled immigrant meet the diversifying world around us in the faces of these new immigrants to our communities. How will we respond to one another? Our responses may be to either insulate ourselves and avoid change or reach out and learn to adapt to these new circumstances. Our faith and religious practices may also need to be reevaluated and reconstructed to meet this new moment. Our families, schools, workplaces, and congregations are also part of that larger global landscape.

The crisis of immigration impacts not just border towns but families living in complex networks of relationships across the country. Immigration and our faithful responses to welcoming the stranger are often very personal. The choice between insulating ourselves from the changing world around us and approaching people who are different from ourselves with curiosity and welcome depends entirely on what the perceived threat is and what might be gained in the process. Barriers of language, dietary practices, religious expectations, and access to familiar everyday items can mean the difference from feeling at home in a foreign place or feeling unwelcome. When we determine to reach beyond our cultural enclave, we must imagine what good may come from this interaction. What is necessary for our survival? If we can see no potential benefit and only potential losses, we will likely become more entrenched in our actions and beliefs that suggest this new person is a threat to our way of life. Yet, if we can see and understand there are benefits for our family and our adult child in this multicultural marriage with this unwelcomed other, then there is hope for a future of changed hearts and minds.

Kamran, who is thirty-four, and Kamalpreet, who is twenty-nine, are a Muslim/Sikh couple, whose national backstories are complicated. Unlike many couples in the United States these days, they do not live together although they are engaged. Kamalpreet lives with her family and will continue to do so until she and Kamran are married. He is the son of Pakistani Indian Muslim parents, and she is a daughter of Indian Punjabi-Sikh parents. The fact that their parents are from the same region in the world does not suggest that they would welcome a marriage between these two. *Sikhs do not marry Muslims.* This couple faced difficulties from both sets of parents, who were resistant to their multicultural interfaith relationship. Kamran was born in the United States. Kamalpreet was born in India. Yet, they are an all-American couple. The story of this newly engaged couple really begins with the story of how their parents immigrated to the United States. Living on the West Coast, both are children of hardworking immigrant families. Their parents faced political unrest in India, which forced both sides to leave their respective countries for better futures—but not before they faced extraordinary challenges that were imposed by larger governmental forces at work.

Kam's father is from Bangladesh, the same territory that was formerly known as East Bengal. That same territory became East Pakistan during the partition of India and then war within and outside of the newly found country caused it to change political leadership again. It was a time of great instability and violence, not unlike we are seeing today. Kam's mother's family was originally from Bihar, a state on the east coast of India not far from the country of Bangladesh. They were forced to leave India in 1947 and immigrated to the newly formed East Pakistan during the partition of India. Kamran tells the story this way, "So my dad is from Bangladesh and my mom, she identifies as Pakistani, but her parents, like a hundred years ago, were from Bihar. But then they'd been displaced multiple times over like multiple civil wars." The borders of India and East and West Pakistan were redrawn in 1947 as part of the British departure from India during their fight for independent rule. Kamran explained in a later interview that East Pakistan, formally East Bengal, was primarily filled with ethnic Bengali people, who have their own distinct culture and language. His family spoke Urdu and were ethnically Indian Muslims. When West Pakistan, the controlling governmental center of the whole of Pakistan, began to oppress ethnic Bengalis, they formed rebel armies and began to actively resist the attempt to unify the divided country under Urdu as the national language. According to Kam's oral history of his family, open fighting and local uprisings began and the Pakistani government sent troops to quell the uprising. Bengali militias expelled Pakistani troops and began to round up Muslim men and put them into concentration camps, while also taking women into the streets and raping and violently killing them, impaling their unborn children. He recounts a story told to him by his mother, who was herself pulled into the street at eleven years old. She watched as a woman of her community was being raped in front of her. All this took place in 1971, forcing his mother's family to flee violence again. Kam's grandmother and mother, along with her two siblings, began a two-month journey crossing the borders of three countries to reach what was West Pakistan, now Pakistan. Their journey took them from the newly independent Bangladesh, into India and Nepal, and then down into Pakistan in 1971. The day after they arrived at their extended families' home, her mother and Kam's grandmother, who had undertaken that impossible journey, suddenly died. Kamran recalls, "My mom was raised by her older siblings until 1984 when she married my dad and came to the United States." Kam's mother's family fled civil wars over two generations as the borders of India, Pakistan, and Bangladesh were being drawn and redrawn by those in power. His family was forced to migrate due to religious and political boundaries being made and remade. It reminds me of a former colleague of mine, who says this about Mexicans in the US, "We didn't cross the border, the border crossed us." Kam's family had the border cross their family multiple times. National identity became reminders of war and strife, migration and fleeing for their lives. Theirs was a history of cultural and religious-based trauma; they did not belong anywhere. Their lives were under constant threats of violence. These are political, institutional powers at work affecting the lives of millions who are caught in the middle of powerful leaders' political firestorms. Kam's story is unfortunately not unique for refugees who flee their war-torn homelands. It is fair to say that he is the son of a political refugee.

GENERATIONAL CONFLICT

Kamalpreet's dad immigrated from the region of Punjab in India, according to her, because of a lack of work opportunities. "There was nothing for him there," she asserts. He did not want to be a farmer like his older brother. How he immigrated to the United States was once a beloved story of the family. Now, her father is reluctant to tell it. This is not surprising given the current climate of immigration and xenophobic political rhetoric in our country. Our borders were more permeable than they are now. We were once more welcoming towards immigrants. Her dad's story is from an earlier time. In her words,

> My dad, who came illegally many, many years ago, over thirty years ago, he has a very crazy story. He hopped on a plane and then crossed the Mexico border to get to the US. I know that he's been legal for thirty years. He got his citizenship. Then he went back to India. He got married to my mom. He went back and forth a few times and when I was three that's when our immigration paperwork was done. And then my mom and I came here. Basically, he went from India to someplace in Germany and he hopped onto a plane in the cargo area with other people.

This is another remarkable story of seeking opportunities and risking everything to pursue a better future. My husband tells me of the hardship that people of Punjab faced after Indira Gandhi, the prime minister of India, was assassinated by her Sikh bodyguards in 1984. Thousands of Sikhs were killed in the aftermath across the country, by some estimates as many as eight thousand.[1] Perhaps Kamalpreet's father was fleeing the pogroms against Sikhs in his country in the aftermath of the prime minister's assassination? I attempted to learn more about her heritage stories, but the details were difficult to come by. What this couple shares are stories of hardship and challenge that cross national boundaries and borders and are based on religious strife between Hindus and Muslims and between Hindus and Sikhs that include persecution and violence. They experienced generational trauma and now seek a brighter future for their own relationship that defies their inherited religious norms. Given the trauma each of their families faced, we will learn later that this couple is interested in letting go of their respective national and religious identities to create something new together.

"Western and Christian" has long been considered by Christian Euro-Americans as what should be the universal organizing principle for the entire world. Samuel Huntington, in *The Clash of Civilizations*, traces the rise

---

1. Pillalamarri, "India's Anti-Sikh Riots."

of "Westernization." Built upon the colonization efforts of capitalistic markets, democratic values, and the Christian religion,[2] Huntington asserts that while the West will continue to remain leaders in technology and science, its global power will wane significantly.[3] That imagined global future of a One World Order that is both Western and Christian will not happen because of the rise of Southeast Asian, Middle Eastern, and Indian markets. "The central problem in the relations between the West and the rest is, consequently, the discordance between the West's—particularly America's—efforts to promote a universal Western culture and its declining ability to do so."[4] The rise in the use of the term "globalization" is really the resulting decline in Western Christian Civilization and a recognition that the increasing cultural and ethnic diversity found within the borders of the United States is because of those rising civilizations exporting both their markets and their talent to the West. Along with their talent however, they export their culture, their identity, their food, their language, *and their religion.*

As these cultures and peoples are imported, so are the historic wars and conflicts that follow them. Huntington delineates *fault line wars* as wars that are between distinct civilizations that are often defined by differences in religions.[5] These kinds of wars, according to Huntington, "tend to be vicious and bloody, since fundamental issues of identity are at stake."[6] The conflict lies in between these two cultures. The problem with our young lovers is not that they are not allowed to love each other; it is, rather, that two cultural communities and religious traditions have not learned how to live with each other without it breaking into conflict and strife every few years. The war at our borders has now come home to dinner. Yet, we still have not learned how to talk with these strangers in our midst without prejudice, misunderstanding, and harboring hate. To welcome the stranger into our family means that we must learn to deal with the centuries of conflict and strife that have beset our community for generations.

Jonathan Sacks, in *The Dignity of Difference*, suggests that while the sins of faith-based colonialization and Westernization may be at the heart of generations of conflict, why not turn to our faiths to help bridge the differences between us? He suggests economic principles from Judaism can

2. Huntington and Brzezinski, *Clash of Civilizations*, 47.
3. Huntington and Brzezinski, *Clash of Civilizations*, 91.
4. Huntington and Brzezinski, *Clash of Civilizations*, 183.
5. Huntington and Brzezinski, *Clash of Civilizations*, 253.
6. Huntington and Brzezinski, *Clash of Civilizations*, 252.

be used to rethink our global economies from one of exploit and export to one that is based on shared responsibility and the concept of *tzedakah*, which refers to "distributive justice" or a combination of both "charity and justice."[7]

> There can be no doubt that more—much more—of the economic surplus of advanced economies should be invested in developing countries to help eradicate extremes of poverty and hunger, ensure universal education, combat treatable disease, reduce infant mortality, improve work conditions and reconstruct failing economies. As with *tzedakah*, the aim should be to *restore dignity and independence to nations as well as individuals*.[8]

Sacks calls on other Jewish concepts to support dignity between diverse cultures and civilizations, such as practicing forgiveness and utilizing the making of covenants to restore hope. He believes that, by making "space for difference," we "can recognize God's image in someone who is not" of our same image. "Can we create a paradigm shift through which we come to recognize that we are enlarged, not diminished, by difference?"[9] Religious and cultural differences then, for Sacks, are not causes for war, but opportunities for growth, especially across religious difference. Rather than the stranger in our midst raising alarms and fears, the stranger could elicit curiosity, collaboration, and the creation of new communities.

---

7. Sacks, *Dignity of Difference*, 113.
8. Sacks, *Dignity of Difference*, 123. Emphasis added.
9. Sacks, *Dignity of Difference*, 201.

5

Intersectionality

IN INDIA MY HUSBAND takes the lead when we travel, go shopping, and especially when we attend religious functions in local Hindu temples. In the United States I typically take the lead when we travel together, go shopping, and especially in the church where I am the minister and head of staff. In each context either of us has more or less power to navigate those situations based on our gender, nationality, culture, and religious belonging. If we were to change the situation to visiting a Christian church in Chennai, I may not take the lead even though I hold status and power in the Christian tradition in the United States. My status as a woman has less power in the highly patriarchal country of India and within the patriarchal Church of South India in particular. So, in that case, my husband, a man who speaks the language, is of Indian origin, and has lived in Chennai would make the introduction of myself to the leadership of the congregation within the Church of South India. He has more assumed power and privilege until they come to know who I am as an ordained minister in the United Church of Christ in the USA. Even as a Hindu man, he serves to legitimatize my role and status within the Christian tradition. Similarly, while in the Chicago suburbs when we attend events at the Hindu temple, my husband who is Hindu will have to navigate questions of my legitimacy of belonging within the temple as a white woman, even when I am wearing a traditional saree and have advanced theological and religious education. Once people come to know that I am not an outsider within religious circles, they will take my presence and participation more seriously. It so happens that over time I gained the leadership's trust. Then I was welcomed as a valued leader, especially when I brought groups of Christian clergy and seminary students to the Hindu Temple in Chicago for immersive educational interfaith experiences. I am seen as a Christian Interfaith leader and am a respected clergyperson in the Indian Hindu context. I work to bridge the cultures between the American Christian religious majority and the Hindu religious minority within the Midwest. My husband and I have more or less power based on our intersecting identities depending on a range of factors, including our race, gender, ethnicity, sexuality, nationality, culture, age, class, caste, the language we speak, and our religion.

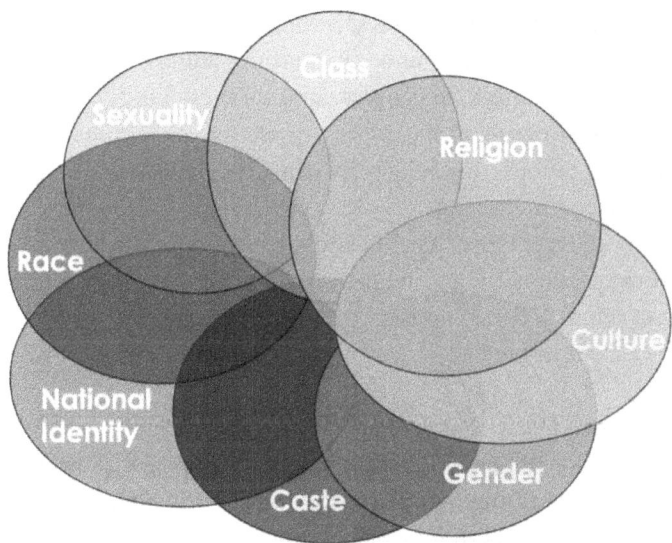

Figure 5.1 Intersectional Identities

Intersectionality[1] is a term that tries to name the complexities of our intersecting identities and the ways that those identities may contribute to greater institutional oppression, discrimination, or bias in particular situations in our life, such as systems of health care, religious institutions, schools, or government settings.[2] Living in the United States, white heterosexual

---

1. The term "intersectionality" was developed and expounded upon by Kimberlé Crenshaw Williams, who explored the impact that race and gender posed on black women within the legal system who were being unfairly treated regarding cases of domestic violence. Williams, "Mapping the Margins."

2. Williams, "Mapping the Margins."

Christian cisgender men tend to have the most power and status granted to them. In India lighter-skinned brown heterosexual Hindu cisgender men of higher castes tend to have the most power and status granted to them. In neither setting do I hold a position where power is automatically granted because of my gender, even though I may have more belonging due to my race, culture, and native language. In India my husband tends to have more power because of his gender, culture, and religious belonging. Yet, where he holds the most power is in his workplace in the Chicago area as a manager of a team of twenty-seven research scientists and technicians where he manages staff, projects, and labs. Different aspects of our identities in various settings allow us more or less belonging and the ability to adapt and navigate those complex systems of relationships and cultural expectations.

Multicultural interfaith couples navigate these kinds of complexities across their identities on a regular basis depending on whose family, workplace, country, culture, and religious setting they may find themselves in. And the person who once had power, privilege and status may find that they have less power to navigate those once familiar settings because of the race, culture, nationality, and religion of their partner. In other words, in the eyes of others in your community you may become less Jewish because you married someone who is not Jewish. This is the case with Adam and Maria.

Adam and Maria, our Jewish/Catholic couple living in Costa Rica, strive to practice both religious traditions daily, celebrate both cultural identities, and speak one another's languages. Their eighteen-month-old son is being raised in both religious traditions and can already pray a traditional Catholic prayer as well as a Hebrew prayer along with his mother and father. He runs into Adam's office to open the drawer and put on his *kippa*, which gives Adam a great deal of pride. Their relationship is the most complex of those I interviewed: crossing national borders of the United States and Costa Rica; spanning two languages both English and Spanish; practicing their respective religious traditions of Reform Judaism and Roman Catholicism; and merging their two diverse cultural traditions, "American" and Costa Rican. Adam is quick to point out that we need to change our language from using "American" when what we really mean is "United States," because Costa Rica is part of the Americas. One of the gifts of their relationship is its complexity. The couple highlights the indivisibility of the intersectional identities of culture, religion, and national origin. To understand what I mean here about their intersectionality is to appreciate that you cannot take Maria's Catholicism out of the culture of Costa Rica, nor can you take Adam's Jewishness out of the culture of the United States. Their identities are culturally, religiously, and nationally complex and interconnected. Together their relationship has added additional layers of complexity as they have learned to adapt and include the traditions of their spouse in one another's life. They have learned so much about one another's religious and cultural traditions that they are becoming not only bilingual and bicultural, but also, they are becoming spiritually fluid;[3] that is to say, they are able to move between Jewish and Catholic spaces with ease while maintaining their own unique identities in the practice of their faith.

When we speak of intersectionality, we are also interested in the ways we talk about God and meaning making within multicultural interfaith couples. The ways they are reimagining their faith practices and remaking their identities is precisely at the heart of intersectional theology. Coauthors Grace Ji-Sun Kim and Susan M. Shaw in *Intersectional Theology* speak to why an intersectional approach to our research and writing is important, and I argue it is important for us to understand the complex forms of discrimination multicultural interfaith couples face on a daily basis in any context. They write,

> With its wider inclusive lens of gender, race, sexual identity, social class, ability, age, and nation, intersectional theology brings the shifting and often invisible structures of power and privilege to the fore and demands attentiveness to social location and the simultaneity of subordinate and dominant identities in our theologizing. With its bias toward justice, in particular, intersectional theology calls us to prioritize the margins and ensure our theologizing moves us toward a more just world by disrupting dominant paradigms and destabilizing structures of power while envisioning a way forward toward God's reign of peace.[4]

When we take into consideration the variety of challenges that these couples face, we also acknowledge that they face different forms of exclusion, micro aggressions, and prejudice than they would if they were alone in a context that reflected their racial background, their culture, or their religious community. Together with their partner, their families and children, they become outsiders in their own communities. They once belonged. Now married to the unwelcome religious other, their claim to insider status

---

3. See Bidwell, *When One Religion*.
4. Kim and Shaw, *Intersectional Theology*, 1115.

is relinquished. By paying attention to the ways our identities bring us more status or power, access or exclusion we can begin to create safe spaces for our multicultural interfaith couples to be welcomed and find belonging.

Sharon Jacob, an Asian American theologian, speaks to the value and importance of taking into account the intersectional identities of persons within their national context. Writing about Asian women in the national context of India she states,

> The quest for equality, liberation, and the ability to lead a life free of violence and assault is an ongoing fight for the average Indian woman. At the same time, while women's bodies have been subject to sexualization, violence, and discrimination, women belonging to marginal religious groups are prone to another added layer of harassment and violence given their already subordinated status in society. Thus, women belonging to Christian and Muslim communities in India, and also women who are Dalits, tribals, poor, and refugees experience double oppression because of their gender as well as their religious and caste identities.[5]

Intersectional identities bring multiple layers of discrimination and oppression especially for women of lower economic status as well as lower castes within the Hindu context. Citing both the problem of the "rise of nationalism on a global scale"[6] and "the Asian American woman as the perpetual foreigner,"[7] she points to the need for our theology to consider the role that politics, class, caste, and gender impact the ways that Asian women may never find safe spaces to be themselves.

Our multicultural interfaith couples face similar challenges where they cannot find religious cultural spaces where they feel fully at home. One or the other within their couple will be the perpetual outsider, to use Jacob's analogy here. Adam does not belong in Catholic spaces even with his wife Maria. Maria does not belong in Jewish spaces even with her husband Adam. Once married, their religious identities merge and they become something new, they are a Jewish-Catholic family that will find it difficult to fully belong in one another's religious communities. That is the unnamed cost of marrying the religious outlaw. Yet, what if our religious spaces were the unwelcoming places, and not the fault of the people who dared to love across difference? There is hope that intersectionality can

---

5. Jacob, "Neither Here nor There!," 124.
6. Jacob, "Neither Here nor There!," 124.
7. Jacob, "Neither Here nor There!," 131.

become a blessing within religious contexts if we are able to pay attention to the ways our institutional biases against the religious other are named and opportunities for inclusion are created.

Usha and Patrick, a UU-Hindu/Catholic-Christian couple living in the Midwest share about residing in an "overbearingly white town." Soon after they married, they moved from the East Coast to the Midwest. Together they had to navigate Usha's religious, cultural, and racial belonging in their new community. Patrick shares, "In our extremely white town that Usha is an Indian American and is willing to engage with other people about being Indian American and being Hindu American has made her, at times, a hot commodity. I am another white guy." Yet her legitimacy for *belonging* in their town is granted by her husband's profession at a local Christian college. When walking in town wearing traditional Indian clothing, she is occasionally asked the question, "Where are you from?" and when she responds New York, they ask again, *"Where are you really from?"* This is a common question asked of people who present as racially, ethnically, or culturally distinct from the community in which they reside. The question is a microaggression in that it first is a distrust of the first answer to the question of where they are from—as in *"you can't be from there because of your difference."* And secondly it signals that the person does not belong in that community, whether because of their race, culture, dress, religious expression, or country of origin.

These microaggressive questions are an example of the kinds of discrimination that multicultural couples may experience. Even as we begin to explore the tensions between a mostly white Christian midwestern town and a woman of Asian heritage who happens also to be Hindu—she is *othered* based on the intersectionality of her race, religion, and culture. Usha's othered status engenders both curiosity as well as prejudice, invitations for cultural exchanges as well as questions of her belonging. She is both welcome and not. The tension between her religious traditions as well as her distinct cultural and racial identities also makes her a potential change agent in her community. What is seen by the community as a detriment can be transformed into a benefit for that same community.

A multicultural interfaith couple embodies an intersectional set of identities[8] that are informed by the complexities of their culture, country of

---

8. See for instance Steinmetz, "She Coined." Law professor Kimberlé Crenshaw coined the term in 1989 to distinguish the unique discrimination black women experience distinct from either black men or white women.

origin, and immigration status as well. We all inhabit intersectional identities, but when we live in a monogamous culture who worships the same, looks the same, and hails from the same place of origin, it is easier to lose those cultural understandings of our own intersectional identities. Multicultural interfaith couples are made aware of distinct intersectional identities because of how they or their partner are more or less welcomed based on each of those overlapping identities. This awareness and their ability to navigate multiple cultural spaces is a particular strength of these couples. How parents of adult children who marry outside of expected religious and cultural norms will reject or, ultimately, welcome their interfaith partner into the larger family will be determined by a host of factors, including theological perspectives, cultural understandings, historical realities, and the role that identity, power, and privilege play out in their context. Traditional understandings of intersectionality focus on the ways that fear and prejudice leads to discrimination and oppression. What if we were to understand our intersectional identities as opportunities for deeper engagement across our differences leading to deeper understanding and growth? We can become agents for change in our communities precisely because we are able to navigate complex cultural, religious, and racialized settings. Then our intersectionality identity transforms from being a burden to becoming a blessing.

6

Dignity and Worth

HUMAN TOUCH IS ONE way we show affection and love. Holding hands, hugging, caresses, kisses on the cheek are a few of the ways families demonstrate connection and belonging. Not touching while in some cultures is a form of respect. In others, it can serve as a way to send powerful messages to people that they do not belong, they are not welcome, or they need to stand back or stay away. We show one another dignity and worth by how we include or exclude them in our everyday interactions, like when we sit down to share a meal together. In this regard the practice of touch*ability* creates community, and those we will not touch delineates those who are outsiders and unclean. Touchability and untouchability are still common physical expressions within Hindu households where ritual purity is practiced, like within my husband's Brahmin family. Ritual purity is a matter of both physical hygiene and spiritual preparedness. On the holiest of days, this practice is called being *muddie*, which, ironically, means the most spiritually clean. Some shower with their clean clothes on to assure that there is no chance of impurity when performing the most important religious rituals, such as celebrating death anniversaries. This concept of ritual purity or spiritual cleanliness matters most when we consider the preparation and the cooking of food and then serving what is prepared. Who cooks the food and who serves the food can either maintain the ritual purity for the elders in the family or contaminate it by how they prepare it or by not being of the accepted members of the household. In our family, belonging in the family means you eat, bathe, pray, cook, and dress according to the religion and customs of the Tamil Iyengar ways. But there is more to it, as I would learn.

Serving our elders their food is an honor and a duty among women in an extended family. The youngest married woman in the family will be tasked with not only preparing the meal but also her duty includes first to serve the eldest in the family the components of their South Indian meal: rice, sambar, and vegetable. We sit cross-legged on the floor to eat together as a family, and we eat with our right hands. The right hand is reserved for serving, which is not possible if you have begun to eat. So, one woman may wait to begin eating until everyone is served and has begun to eat their second course so she can conveniently serve the family.

In 2000 we made a big trip to India while we were expecting our second child. I was very pregnant, nearly eight months along. Our little fifteen-month-old son was the darling of the family, the eldest grandchild, a little Krishna running around. We were all together, the food was laid out, we all sat down cross-legged along with *Amma*'s mother, who was the eldest in the home. She is our *paati*, which, in Tamil, means grandmother. As was my duty and honor, I reached across the prepared items and picked up the ladle to serve everyone who was seated. As my hand approached *paati*'s plate with sambar, a hot lentil stew, she flinched away from me and prevented me from serving her. At first, I thought she did not want sambar. But then her daughter served her. Then I knew instantly what was wrong. It was me. In that moment she considered me unclean to serve her because I was not born into the Iyengar caste. No amount of cultural learning, bathing, wearing a saree, South Indian cooking, or Hindu religious practices could have overcome that barrier. I felt hot with anger at the injustice of it all. She did not want food from the ladle that my hand touched. I was impure in her eyes. Infuriated, I grabbed my son's little arm and showed her and pointed, "The same blood that runs through his veins is the same blood that is in mine. Is he impure in your eyes? Can he touch you? If he can, then why can't I?" I stood up, big baby belly and all, took my plate of food and in disgust threw it out. Everyone was upset by what happened, but for different reasons. My husband was caught in the middle. He understood what happened and was hurt by how his *paati* had treated me. I was humiliated and felt she was ashamed of me. My dignity was lost.

The desire to belong to a community, to a family, to have dignity and feel valued are essential aspects of what it means to be human. We desire to be treated fairly and to contribute to the world around us. Multicultural interfaith couples may for the first time see their own loss of dignity and worth in their family because of who they love. Or they may see that their chosen partner is not valued or regarded because of their religious tradition, the color of their skin, their culture, or even their national origin. In short, strong messages of *you don't belong here* may be communicated by the very people whom you have grown to love. The religious or cultural community who once welcomed the individual may now shun the same person and their partner because of whom they chose to marry. Some may even face fears of being disinherited from their families. Some are cut off completely. The pain is real.

Howard Thurman, in *Jesus and the Disinherited*, understands the power of exclusion and hate to gnaw at the soul of the individual. Thurman explores the impact of racism against Black Americans in this still relevant work first published in 1949. He writes, "The masses of men live with their back constantly against the wall. They are the poor, the disinherited, the dispossessed. What does our religion say to them?"[1] What does our faith have to say to our own families who struggle to argue that their partner should be welcomed and treated with dignity? Christian triumphalism continues to be linked with not only racist but also xenophobic rhetoric. Yet even in Thurman's case, it was being questioned by a Hindu that compelled him to examine Christianity's response to the rampant racism and discrimination in the United States and led him to recontextualize Jesus as a Jew in the territory of now Palestine. Thurman quotes his colleague's admonishment, "I am a Hindu. I do not understand. Here you are in my country, standing deep within the Christian faith and tradition. I do not wish to seem rude to you. But, sir, I think you are a traitor to all the darker peoples of the earth."[2] Thurman's book was an answer to his colleague's charge.

Thurman is not the only Christian leader to find prophetic leadership emerging from interfaith encounters with *othered* people. Rev. Dr. Martin Luther King Jr., in his "Palm Sunday Sermon on Mohandas K. Gandhi," shares at length the Christian values of love and nonviolence exhibited by Gandhi. King writes,

> And strangely enough, this little man came in with no armies, no guards around him, no military might, no beautiful clothes, just loin cloth, but this man proved to be the greatest conqueror that the British Empire faced. He was able to achieve, through love and nonviolence, the independence of his people and break the

---

1. Thurman, *Jesus and the Disinherited*, 3.
2. Thurman, *Jesus and the Disinherited*, 5.

backbone of the British Empire. 'Ye shall do greater works than I have done.' And this is exemplified in the life of Mahatma Gandhi.[3]

Multicultural families engage in interfaith dialogue in their everyday encounters as they navigate holidays, religious education, cultural expectations around work and family, as well as rituals surrounding birth and death. Yet something as simple as a lunchtime meal with an intergenerational multicultural family can become a battle ground for dignity and worth. When conflict erupts during these unexpected moments, we see how high the stakes are for the family. Because of the conflict, traditional values and outdated practices are revealed for the harm they cause. While painful for all involved, the conflicts show the impact that the discrimination embedded in the culture and religion impose on the *religious other* in the family. The next generation sees the toll those practices take out on the bodies and spirits of the ones they dearly love. Yet with love and perseverance these events can be transformed to bridge cultures in the family. My husband's father, whom we call *Appa*, was not present for the incident at lunch. When he returned, he went on a walk with his son who detailed the events that led to the palpable tension in the house. Later that day while I was still sulking, my husband took me up to the roof terrace and shared with me what *Appa* told him. *Appa* was aware of the caste bias in his mother-in-law's beliefs. "These old people don't realize what they are doing. She had a right to be upset by *paati's* actions." *Appa* affirmed my right to belong. He restored my dignity in the family. I belonged again, but the wound was there.

When a person is being denied both dignity and belonging, how can they respond? In the case of multicultural interfaith couples, it is often the partner of the *othered* member that helps to create within them the sense that they are *somebody* and that they belong in the family. They advocate for their partner *as somebody* worthy of being in the family. For some this can be a transformative experience going deep into the heart of one's identity. This is certainly true in my own case. Until I felt accepted and loved by my husband and saw how he advocated for me within his own family, there was a nagging sense of shame and fear that I was not only not worthy of love but also that I did not belong anywhere. To know intellectually that you are somebody in God's eyes is not enough. It must be felt from the inside as well as the outside. It must be experienced through and through within a community that declares dignity, belonging, and ultimate worth. Multicultural interfaith couples often struggle against prejudices across race,

3. King, "Palm Sunday Sermon," 31–32.

religion, culture, and national origin to proclaim the dignity and worth of not only their partners but, ultimately, for the dignity and worth of others who have been deemed *the stranger* as well.

In many cases these couples are so concerned about being shunned, ridiculed, or worse that they hide their relationships from their parents. One couple, when it became time to share the news with the family, puts it this way, "When he first came out to his family, it was probably the biggest tension because it took him all summer, literally the whole summer to work up the kind of courage to talk to his dad." Others talk about hiding entire parts of their lives from their families. "I had to hide who [I was]. I had to be a certain way to conform, right? You gotta be guarded in what you share and how you share it and who you hurt and what you say, and all of these things." These amazing young couples in love, at the same time, are dealing with shame and fear of rejection. They understand that because who they love is from a different race, class, caste, religion, or nationality than their family of origin, they risk losing their own belonging. Who they are and who they love becomes a matter of their own dignity and worth also.

Married for more than thirty years in India, Arundhati and Sanjaya, a Christian woman married to a Lingayat Hindu-Atheist man, navigated a tough road of cultural prejudices, religious exclusion, and familial misunderstandings. While both culturally Indian, their religious and caste differences were large barriers within their family. Arundhati struggled to have her identity as a Christian honored by her in-laws. Her Lingayat Hindu-Atheist husband fought for her to be treated with dignity in the family by his parents. Ultimately this worked. Sanjaya's mother stopped pressuring Arundhati to convert to their Hindu religion. By their own willingness to stand up for one another and share their relationship journey with their extended family, others in Sanjaya's family who were finding partners outside of the religion sought out this couple's advice and support. Through persistence and advocacy for one another, Arundhati and Sanjaya have gained the regard and respect of their community. They not only found status together, but they have also helped others navigate the changing religious and cultural landscape within their own diverse community in South India.

Their commitment to honor the dignity and worth of one another was noticed by other members of their family, especially when these members began to make their own choices of life partners outside of the family's religious community. Further, Arundhati and Sanjaya felt compassion for their families because they understood that these nontraditional partners would challenge the values and threaten the expectations from their own parents. Thus, Arundhati and Sanjaya, a multicultural interfaith couple, had the ability to accept people that are *religiously or culturally othered* within their larger social circles. They knew what it was like to not belong and how to navigate those complex social situations. In fact, Sanjaya's family more readily accepted the multicultural and interfaith marriages that occurred in the family in subsequent years. He recalls, "After we got married, several of my cousins left and they got married interreligiously within the Hindu community to a different language or a different caste. And one of my uncles had told [me], 'It all started because of you,' and pointed out to me." Their social change advocacy, while not necessarily intended to change their community standards of acceptability or inclusion of others, did pave the way for additional *outsiders* to be welcomed more quickly into the family circle.

Their social change advocacy did not stop with their families. Sanjaya is not afraid to speak his mind. "If somebody says something about me or anybody, I just go and confront them. 'What the hell are you talking about?' So, if they say anything about my wife or her religion, I say, 'What the hell? What's wrong with you?'" Advocating for the rights of others has been a part of his life and profession as well. He is a longtime peace activist who worked for disarmament and development. He explains, "On issues of disarmament, it was *disarm for development*. You disarm, you reduce your military budgets and then you use the same money, which you're diverting from military into development, and we will become a massive great country." The cause of disarmament is an economic argument for the rights of the poor in his country. For both Sanjaya and Arundhati, religion should not be a factor in determining one's worth or dignity. Describing his essential ethical principles toward others he states, "But it's accepting [people] as people are. Whoever we interact with, we interact with them like humans, it's nothing to do with religion." A person's status or economic background should not matter either. They advocate for the rights of the human being, doing their best to treat everyone with equal dignity and regard. Arundhati continues, "Religion doesn't have a place. And I think economics has no place. Doesn't matter if you're very rich or very poor. I think people are just people."

For Sanjaya and Arundhati, they have navigated a relationship that holds in harmony Arundhati's deep Christian faith and participation in her religious community and Sanjaya's atheism, which also allows for his cultural participation in his family's Hindu practices. His social change advocacy comes from a deep commitment to his country and that country's values. They both value one another's viewpoints and traditions. They both are social change agents. Their advocacy work, in some part, is derived from having to stand up for their partner in context where their beliefs or practices were not the norm. This is a common skill among multicultural interfaith couples.

7

Identity and Belonging

SHIVA AND COLLEEN BROKE off their relationship because, if they stayed together, it would interfere with the tradition of arranged marriages in his family's culture. Staying with Colleen in a "love marriage" was going to cause long-term damage to Shiva's relationship with his parents. Shiva did not want to cause himself or his parents pain by going against the family's religious practices. Yet, during the separation from Colleen, Shiva became disenchanted about who he was and who he wanted to become. This life-defining moment led him to make a different choice. He began to examine which cultural identity he wanted to claim as his own. Would he keep the culture of his family and his childhood or adopt the culture he immigrated to for his graduate studies and where he met the woman he loved? Which culture would he call home?

For Shiva, and many individuals inside of multicultural interfaith families, it feels like an "either-or" kind of decision. The choice was between adopting the Western culture as his own or holding onto his South Asian Indian Hindu way of life. Shiva explains, "What identity do I want to pick? Thus far I had been a very 'conforming to society' kind of person—conforming to my family's wishes and not necessarily rocking the boat too much. Although I had a life that they did not know about, my family. Do I continue with that identity, or do I continue with more what the US is?" He was beginning to grapple with which culture he would find his belonging in long-term. His identity was connected to where he called home and whom he would choose to marry.

Identity and Belonging

Shiva is not alone in his deliberations about his identity. The interplay between religion, class, caste, race, and culture are so strong that when you love someone whose traditions, culture, race, and religion are vastly different from your own, it triggers an identity crisis that takes time to sort out. For a few of the couples I interviewed, this process took months, for another couple it took years. In Shiva's case he speaks of the emotional pain he endured during this period in his life, "It was easier to break up, take the easier route, but not really easy. 'Cause then it was very painful too. Then there was a period of growth and we got back together, and I said, 'Okay. I guess I'm ready to blow it up with my family.'" He understands the risk, but he believes he belongs with Colleen and therefore he chooses to live within the Western cultural way of life.

Shiva used the phrase, "blow it up with my family" twice during our interview. He imagined that telling his family about his relationship with Colleen would cause an explosion. He believed this is something that could cause lasting damage to his parents. Love marriages in traditional Indian Hindu households cause a great deal of pain—not just for the couple, but for the parents, their younger siblings, and, most especially, in the community of the families living in India. Survival within the tight-knit closed culture of a religiously orthodox Hindu community is often dependent on relationships with neighbors, friends, and family who live in the community. Adherence to cultural and religious norms signal belonging and form networks that can make living within the harsh realities of India easier or more difficult. When the network of relationships is strong, the challenges created by flooding, power outages, and water cutoffs are more easily navigated with the support of one's family and friends. Shiva's parents believed their status and belonging would be weakened by their son marrying outside of the caste and community.

One's status within a community is built, in part, on the family's reputation and how well adult children have married within the community. Matters of pride and shame rise and fall with the accomplishments of married children, grandchildren, and the parents' ability to pass on the religious and cultural traditions across the generations. Shiva felt "torn between these two identities" and, ultimately, he began to see that what he valued from his own family and what Colleen valued were more similar than not. "At some point there was a choice to be made because the more I found out about her, the more she occurred to me as a more Eastern philosophy, Indian kind of person. We've got a lot of similarities in terms of how we view things and her openness to learning about the culture and her interest in everything." At this point he makes the decision tell his parents about his relationship with Colleen.

Multicultural interfaith couples, given their religious multiplicity, dual-cultural communities, and racial heritages, as well as national origins, face great challenges with regards to identity and belonging. Particularly in the early years of a relationship as their couple identity is being formed, the individuals within these couples may face prejudice, stereotyped assumptions, fearful remarks, hateful rhetoric, and discriminatory practices from family, colleagues, friends, and community members. These obstacles are designed to dissuade, prevent, or block the couple from either forming or being welcomed into their families, and respective religious and cultural communities. These combined forms of racial, cultural, and religious tensions, which are designed to prevent outsiders from entering the community, may alternatively provide opportunities for growth, resilience, and social transformation. What is intended to harm may in fact create an adaptive response.

Interfaith relationships can help one to become even clearer about one's identity. Another couple living in a large city in Southern India faced similar circumstances: Arundhati and Sanjaya. Arundhati's commitment to her identity as a Christian is strengthened in the face of her in-laws' objections. Arundhati and Sanjaya faced challenges with regards to religion and caste. Sanjaya, her husband, was raised in a very traditional *Lingayat* Hindu family. Lingayat Hindus were established in the twelfth century as an anti-Brahmin sect within the Shaivite tradition—those who worship Shiva and the symbolic *Shivalingam*.[1] Arundhati, his wife, faced pressure from her mother-in-law to convert in a simple ceremony where they would put a lingam necklace on her. She recalls her mother-in-law saying, "It's nothing. You don't need to wear it all the time." Arundhati's response was, "No. I have been Christian, and this is part of my identity." Yet this was not enough to dissuade her mother-in-law. The pressure to convert arose in a conversation about the religion of their future child; Arundhati was pregnant at the time. In an act of solidarity and advocacy, her new husband came downstairs and shouted at his mother, "The baby's not even born and you're going on like this? We will all become Muslims!" This threat of converting to Islam from the Hindu context is considered to be worse than being married to a Christian. It is common in my own local Hindu community of friendships

---

1. "Lingayats."

to hear this sentiment repeated this way: "My children can marry anyone they want as long as they are not Muslim or gay." While homophobic and Islamophobic, what they are trying to say is that caste does not matter; the parent is not going to follow the traditional practices of arranging their child's marriage, and if their child falls in love on their own that will be fine as long as *they are not gay and their chosen partner is not Muslim*. Imagine how much more difficult it is for multicultural interfaith couples who are gay or trans or who do not fit the cisgender heterosexual norm to share their true selves with their families. Unfortunately, like many queer couples, these prejudices keep their lives and their relationships hidden all the more. In Sanjaya's case, his threat shouted at his mother was enough to silence her and end once and for all the pressure his family was putting on his wife to convert to his family's religion. Arundhati retained her Christian identity, her husband demanded his family respect that identity, and he protected his wife's dignity. Subsequently Sanjaya's mother began to adjust to this new reality of having a Christian daughter in-law as a part of the family.

FINDING BELONGING AFTER THE STRUGGLE

When multicultural interfaith couples remain committed to their religious and cultural identity over time, whether newly defined like Shiva or reaffirmed like Arundhati, this act of self-differentiation may lead to compassion, understanding, acceptance and, finally, belonging in the family that previously shunned, excluded, or criticized them. Arundhati was troubled and became emotional as she reflected on the behavior of her in-laws when she was in the early years of her relationship with Sanjaya. She shows great compassion for them. She recalls how difficult it was for her parents-in-law. "I was a beef-eating Christian, definitely an untouchable." For her family to come to accept her, even as an Indian Christian, in their household meant confronting daily religious rituals centering around their status and caste. She remembers, "For a year or so [my mother-in-law] was a little upset because of my joining the family; they lost caste. And because of my cooking and them eating what I cooked, they lost caste." To say they *lost caste* is a statement about acceptability, status, and belonging; within the community, they lost standing because their son married an *outsider*. Her husband, a Hindu-Atheist does not adhere to these standards of caste or ritual purity. Sanjaya rejected the traditionalism of his parents' religious orthodoxy and, instead, identifies as an atheist. Jokingly, Arundhati, when asked what Hindu holidays they celebrate together, states, "Sanjaya eats, he does not celebrate." However, Arundhati values "the strong goddess presence" in her husband's faith tradition yet rejects "their extreme belief in caste and the strong patriarchy despite the goddesses." Together they have shared cultural values and distinct religious practices.

Being a Christian/Hindu couple in India is quite different than being a Christian/Hindu couple in the United States. The power dynamics are switched. In the US, American Christianity is the dominant religious tradition and Hinduism is *othered*. In India, Hinduism is overwhelmingly the dominant religious tradition, and, like in the US with the rise of Christian nationalism, Hindu nationalism has taken over party politics and rules neighborhood sentiments. There is a rising sentiment among some people in India that to be *culturally Indian* you need to be Hindu. If you are of another religious tradition, as in the case of Arundhati as Christian, then your Indian identity becomes suspect. Arundhati shared a minor example of this in her family: "My mother-in-law used to say, 'Oh, so you do *that* in *your house* also? Just like us Indians,' and I would say, 'What are you saying? I've always been an Indian. I'm an Indian, you're a Hindu. I'm a Christian, but we are both Indian.' Then my mother-in-law would say, 'Yes, yes, yes. I keep forgetting. Sorry.'" At once belonging and then suddenly not belonging is common within these families. Navigating that *outsider* status is ever present.

When asked about this mistaken identity in Sanjaya's family, the couple responded that they believe it originated from his parents' earlier interactions with British Christians, who worked in a nearby textile company. An association was made early in her mother-in-law's mind that Christian indicates *foreign*. For Arundhati, who lives openly as a Christian, attends the Church of South India, and sings in the choir, the fact that she is accepted within her husband's family is a big deal. Her husband's advocacy on her behalf made all the difference. He explains, "She doesn't pass as Hindu at all. She goes around as Christian. There's no question on that. She is a practicing Christian, and all my relatives and friends know that she's teaching at [a local Christian college]." Arundhati maintains her Christian identity within her larger Hindu family and culture, but not without facing implicit biases that implicate a sense of *religious otherness*.

Getting to the point of being welcomed and feeling like she belonged took many years. For more than ten years, Arundhati studied all the religious Lingayat rituals; she learned to cook the traditional recipes and how to celebrate the various Hindu festivals. Even while continuing to practice her own Christian tradition, she took the time to learn the many names for the various deities—both Gods and Goddesses that her husband's family worshiped throughout the seasons of the year. With such devotion and discipline, she ultimately changed the hearts and minds of her husband's family. Speaking tenderly of her mother-in-law as "a lady of great intelligence and dignity," Arundhati recalls, "years later I asked my mother-in-law, 'All of you are so orthodox, how did you agree to this marriage between your eldest darling son and me?' And she said, 'If I said 'no' I'd have lost him. Is that smart?'" Arundhati's mother-in-law died sometime later. Yet the memory of those tensions still arise between herself and her sister-in-law, who continues to support those traditional "caste-ist" ways. Despite those occasional reminders of their religious differences, Arundhati now claims Sanjaya's family as her family. This is a remarkable change in community attitudes on both sides. She concludes, "He has a very large family and are fairly close-knit. And I must say that after about seven or eight years had gone by, I suddenly realized that they were my family too, you know?" *Belonging* changes one's status from being *the other* and outsider to the family to being among and within the family. Your identity is bound together with the family and the family's identity is now bound to yours.

LETTING GO OF RELIGIOUS IDENTITY

Kamalpreet and Kamran are of the generation of people who are becoming less religious. He shares that he rarely goes to the mosque anymore. He has attended services at Kamalpreet's *gurudwara* more frequently, reserving his attendance at mosques to weddings and funerals. They are less interested in the performance of their religious identities in the public space. Kamalpreet explains that her family was not that religiously adherent: "Growing up, we weren't at the *gurudwara* every single Sunday. My parents had to work. My mom worked the night shift. My dad worked the day shift. So, you know, what were you supposed to do?" Her dad does not wear the turban; they cut their hair, which adherent Sikhs do not; only she and her mom wear the *kara*, the silver bangle that is one of the five K's[2] of Sikhism.[3] Kamalpreet got her kara from the Golden Temple, the most holy place for Sikhs in India. She believes in the values of Sikhism, which include equality for women and a genuine care for all of life as well as the earth's creatures.

> My mom is the best. If she sees a spider, she's not going to go kill it. She literally will pick it up in a little paper towel and put it outside. While the rest of us are like, 'no, kill it.' Even my dad, he's like 'you shouldn't do this—that's going to hurt someone or that's going to harm somebody.' I feel like that's been instilled in me since I was very young.

Yet when thinking about their future with children, they are more interested in the values of their traditions and the common cultural heritage than of their distinctive religious identities. Kamalpreet explains it this way, "After my parents' generation passes away, who's going to remember any of this? I don't even know half of it. Kamran knows more of the history because he likes to read about different things, but I don't know anything and that's supposed to be my roots. I don't see the next generation even having a problem with it. When Kamran and I go places, they're like, oh yeah, they're just, they're both Indian." She believes that their shared Indian ancestral heritage—*in other words, their race*—will be what will define them in the public eye, not the performance of their religious identities. She may be right; perhaps they will find their belonging not in their countries of origin or their religious upbringing but rather in their shared culture. In this way they are choosing together a shared identity.

CHOOSING RELIGIOUS CONVERSION

Paul and Cathy are a Buddhist-Catholic/Buddhist couple who have invested a great deal of their religious life and activism in the justice movements within El Salvador. Cathy was a former Catholic who was divorced and, because of that, her relationship with Paul faced many outside obstacles. Yet it was her own deep questioning that inspired a religious transformation for herself and, ultimately, would impact the couple in profound ways. It

---

2. The five symbols of Sikhism are items which worn by adherent members of the tradition. These are Kesh-uncut hair, Kirpan-small sword, Kara-steel bangle, Kangha-wooden comb, and Kachera-cotton undergarment. To learn more about the 5 K's see for instance Sikhism Guide, "Five Sikh Symbols."

2. Rowell, "Sikhism," 161–80.

began with questions of who she was and where she belonged. Questions of religious identity were central for Cathy as she began to look more deeply at Buddhism for answers that Christianity could not satisfy. She describes this process as *breaking open*. "In '91 we had spent about six months in India. I had some really powerful experiences. We had our kids with us and a dear friend, another Buddhist, and we sat under the Bo Tree in Bodh Gaya together. It got me thinking about myself and many different things. After coming back from India, I went through a really difficult kind of breaking open." Her move out of the Catholic tradition and into the Buddhist tradition was more of a realigning of her true sense of self and her beliefs around the innate goodness in people. She found healing in the process of finding her belonging within the Buddhist teachings of Pema Chodron. "I found it difficult to reinsert myself into my old life. I really struggled with my Catholic faith, even more than I had before. Earlier I had struggled with the sexism in the church, language in the church, sexist language. [Pema Chodron] really spoke to me, her Buddhist teaching. Especially about buddha nature and that innate goodness and love is present. Nothing we have to strive for, it's there." Well-known Buddhist monk and teacher Pema Chodron is a woman and spoke to Cathy's need to find acceptance and goodness within herself and others. Her previous concerns with the institutionalized sexism within the Catholic Church carried over into her Buddhism, as she was wary of the improper student/teacher relationships. This is why, when she first took Buddhist refuge, it was with a group of women who were meeting weekly and studying Pema Chodron's teachings together. Breaking with tradition of taking vows with a teacher, Cathy explains, "we took vows to each other." Together they were adapting the practices to fit with their feminist understanding—a move toward inclusion and justice one might argue. Cathy's identity shifted from being an uncomfortable Catholic to a centered and grounded Buddhist. She found belonging in her feminist Buddhist community. This all took place during her marriage to Paul Knitter, a renowned Catholic pluralist theologian. Their journey was not easy. They faced a great deal of institutional resistance when they decided to marry.

8

Expanding Identities and Double Belonging

GEETHA AND PETER ARE a newly married interracial interfaith couple. Geetha identifies as an Indian American and culturally Hindu. Her parents immigrated to the United States before she was born. She was raised in a Tamil Hindu culture in Northern California. She speaks both English and Tamil. Peter came to the United States for school from Taiwan. His father is a Taiwanese Evangelical Christian minister. He speaks both English and his family's language, Mandarin. Peter still identifies as Christian, but his beliefs have changed. In the process of sharing with one another about their different religious beliefs and practices, they have grown to be more open and accepting of one another's culture, food preferences, and religious practices. Peter has let go of some of the more exclusivist beliefs of Taiwanese Evangelicals that suggest non-Christians are excluded from God's salvation. He learned about other expressions of Christianity, which espouse progressive theology and have a more welcoming view of other religious traditions. "My whole perspective of Christianity as a religion changed. It is no longer this very Evangelical box. Before, you were always taught this is the only way to think about it. If you think about it another way, that is heretical. But, then, you start to realize that it is not true at all. You can still believe in Christianity and still be respectful and still appreciate other religions." While Peter's Christian faith has become more progressive, Geetha's views of vegetarianism, derived from her Hindu culture, has expanded to be more inclusive of her husband's Taiwanese food preferences. He eats meat. She is a lifelong vegetarian and comes from a family of strict vegetarians. Their multicultural interfaith journey as a married couple is expanding their cultural and religious identities. Both are learning more about their traditions because they have to explain their beliefs and rituals to their partner. Geetha shared, "We have definitely learned from one another. I probably wouldn't know as much about my own culture if I hadn't been dating him. He doesn't know anything about Tamil Brahmin Hinduism. I feel like I have to educate myself in order to pass on that information." This is not unusual in multicultural interfaith couples. At the center of these changes is their deep and profound love for one another and for their families. The most interesting part of their young relationship is their commitment to stand up for their partner's beliefs and food preferences with disapproving family or community members. Their identities are expanding. They are becoming committed to one another's religious expressions. As they attend religious functions together, they may find there are aspects of their partner's faith or tradition that they find resonate with their new sense of self. In the process they may develop a new expansive identity that has more than one religious or cultural origin. They may find that their spiritual roots are reaching in new directions toward the cultural territory of their beloved. While Geetha and Peter do not individually claim dual religious identities, there are couples within the multicultural interfaith category who, over time, grow to find belonging in their partner's traditions as well as their own.

Identity plays an important role in spiritual rootedness. Learning to name and claim multiple religious identities can be a life-long process. In the case of some of the multicultural interfaith couples in this study, multiple religious belonging comes as a result of the merging of their two faith traditions. They attend each other's places of worship, plan sacred ceremonies together, or explore deeper meanings within one another's traditions. Over time they may feel as connected to their second religious tradition as they do to the tradition they brought into the marriage. Yet there are risks with sharing the fullness of one's interfaith identity. Duane Bidwell, in *When One Religion Isn't Enough*, delineates another type of religious multiplicity as *spiritual fluidity*. In his book he talks about the risks of being religiously authentic:

> Disclosing multiplicity carries enormous risk. Spiritually fluid people often feel anxious when deciding whether to hide or disclose their religious multiplicity. Hiding it can protect them from judgment, conflict with others, and the need to justify themselves.

But concealing multiplicity also compromises their honesty and authenticity; they're unable to be vulnerable with people they care about, especially family and religious leaders.[1]

As multicultural interfaith couples make the decision of when and how to disclose who they wish to marry to their two families of origin, this can begin the formation of a more complex identity for both partners. They are choosing to become more than who they have been, and this often involves claiming, in some respect, a connection to their partner's religious tradition. The risks for sharing these new "braided identities"[2] can be very high, bringing unwanted questions of legitimacy and professional standing upon those who dare to be completely authentic. "Scholars and religious leaders almost demand that spiritually fluid people justify themselves, logically and doctrinally, against criteria established by European philosophy, Christian theology, and the academic industry that produces 'legitimate' knowledge."[3] In my interfaith story, my desire to serve as an ordained minister was questioned repeatedly by ordination bodies, which suggested that the legitimacy of my call to Christian ministry was suspect not because of my spiritual fluidity, which I would never have shared at that point, but simply because I married someone who was religiously othered—especially someone who was Hindu. If there was little room for love across religious traditions, imagine how these same ordination bodies would have responded to an authentic sharing of the ways in which our family felt a double rootedness in our multiple religious belonging?

PRACTICING BOTH RELIGIONS

Susan Katz Miller, in her book *Being Both: Embracing Two Religions in One Interfaith Family*, looks at the gifts that come from families celebrating and educating their children within both of their parents' religious traditions.[4] Miller, herself a child of parents from two different religions, was not able to be raised in both religions because of the limitations placed on her parents, especially from the Jewish tradition, which would not support a dual-faith home. She was raised entirely Jewish, yet when she got to college,

---

1. Bidwell, *When One Religion*, 57.
2. Bidwell, *When One Religion*, 51.
3. Bidwell, *When One Religion*, 50.
4. Miller, *Being Both*.

her faith and practice was not enough for her to be considered *fully Jewish* because her mother was Episcopalian.⁵ Within Jewish households there can be reluctance and suspicion of practicing Christians because of years of anti-Semitic discrimination by a predominately Christian culture. Within Orthodox and Conservative Jewish traditions, one's connection to full participation in the religious tradition and belonging within that community is believed to be passed on through the mother. Therefore, if your mother is not Jewish, in some circles, regardless of being raised within the tradition, you are not considered to belong to that faith community. She was not *Jewish enough*.

Many families within multiple religious and cultural identities are often deemed *not enough*. My children, for instance, were not *Indian enough*. When Miller approached her rabbi to arrange her marriage to her Christian husband, she confronted the same prejudice as her parents did years before when her rabbi said, "I can't touch this." Miller states that those words effectively "labeled my marriage as something untouchable."⁶ Her book details a grassroots movement among Jewish/Christian families across the country who refused to deny either one of their spouses' religious traditions and choose, instead, to celebrate *both religions* and raise their children as Jewish and Christian. A variety of organizations organically developed in Chicago, New York, San Francisco, and Washington, DC, that, ultimately, come together within the "Interfaith Family Network" and I became aware of their Facebook presence through Miller's blog *Being Both*.

Miller argues that raising children in both traditions provides "literacy in both religions," promotes "cultural harmony," and creates a "revolution" of "interfaith pride."⁷ Arguing for the gifts of being both, she suggests that these dual identities actually create stronger individuals, who no longer adhere to strict binary views of the world.⁸ "In choosing to raise our children with interfaith identities, we join a growing societal rebellion against being forced to choose one race, one culture, even one gender."⁹ Drawing on Maria Root's work on multiracial identity, Miller adapts her "Bill of Rights for People of Mixed Heritage" to include rights of "Interfaith People," which states, among other things, "I have the right not to justify my existence

---

5. Miller, *Being Both*, 10.
6. Miller, *Being Both*, 12.
7. Miller, *Being Both*, 46–50.
8. Miller, *Being Both*, 51.
9. Miller, *Being Both*, 51.

in this world; not to keep the races (or religions) separate within me; and not to justify my ethnic (or religious) legitimacy."[10] When I shared the entire bill of rights, which included both the terms "races" and "religions" therein, my daughter asked me if I had written it. She heard echoes of our own interfaith family, Hindu and Christian, in this Bill of Rights and found herself reflected as a biracial interfaith adult child herself. Miller validates adapting existing rituals as well as innovating new rituals to fit the needs of interfaith families. For example, she shares the liturgy of an interfaith baby-welcoming ceremony that builds on the traditions within both the Jewish and Christian faiths by celebrating the many senses of the child through a series of *blessings*. "Bless our children's minds with intelligence and wisdom. Bless their eyes so they will see great vistas. . . . Bless their mouths for the enjoyment of tasting and talking. . . . Bless their arms for embracing friendship and love."[11] The gifts of Miller's book are many for interfaith families seeking to find both legitimacy and validation to practice the multiple religious traditions of their families.

SPIRITUAL FLUIDITY

Duane Bidwell, formally a professor of practical theology and spiritual care at Claremont School of Theology, brings a whole new dimension to our conversation of religious diversity as he shares the gifts of spiritual fluidity. Bidwell explains that spiritually fluid people, created either by inheriting, choosing, or receiving another tradition, come to relate to and function within more than one religion. They may be connected intellectually and/or through religious practices to two different traditions like Buddhist Christians, where we would locate former Catholic priest, Christian theologian, and Buddhist practitioner Paul Knitter or Hindu Christians like theologian and philosopher Raimundo Panikkar. Double belonging is a greater commitment to two traditions where one's identity is found within both traditions. Borrowing from W. E. B. Du Bois's concept of *double consciousness*,[12] Bidwell argues that spiritually fluid people gain greater insight into the world's problems. "Because you live in two realities, you see things with more complexity. You are always aware of context and the ways that larger

---

10. Miller, *Being Both*, 52.
11. Miller, *Being Both*, 132.
12. See Du Bois, "Strivings of the Negro People."

Expanding Identities and Double Belonging

social systems shape how others perceive and receive you."[13] W. E. B. Du Bois says it this way in his article in *The Atlantic* in 1897,

> It is a peculiar sensation, this double-consciousness, this sense of always looking at one's self through the eyes of others, of measuring one's soul by the tape of a world that looks on in amused contempt and pity. One feels his two-ness,—an American, a Negro; two souls, two thoughts, two unreconciled strivings; two warring ideals in one dark body, whose dogged strength alone keeps it from being torn asunder. The history of the American Negro is the history of this strife,—this longing to attain self-conscious manhood, to merge his double self into a better and truer self.[14]

Similarly, spiritually fluid people have insight into two worlds, are able to code switch, pass, and live with this double consciousness either publicly or privately depending on the power, privilege and legitimacy they may have within the circles of influence where they operate. Like Dubois references, there can also be a feeling of angst that these multiple consciousnesses cannot be reconciled. Our multicultural interfaith couples may be considering when they belong or do not belong; when their race, culture, or religion is perceived to be inside or outside of the context they find themselves within. They often navigate when they are *an insider* and when they are *an outsider*. Their behaviors, languages spoken, clothing, cultural expressions will vary based on the appropriate context. Over time this ability to easily move between spaces and cultures can become a blessing rather than a burden. Multicultural interfaith couples use these cultural adaptations to navigate various religious contexts so that their belonging in those spaces is less questioned. As they master this ability, they learn important leadership skills, including cultural sensitivity and the ability to build relationships in diverse communities. Moving from one context to the other becomes easy for families that regularly move between both religious and cultural spaces. I found this to be true within the couples I interviewed.

Long before I went to seminary, a friend recommended to me a book by the Zen Buddhist teacher Thich Nhất Hạnh, *Living Buddha, Living Christ*. It was the first time I felt validated for having more than one spiritual tradition that spoke to me deeply and profoundly. Nhất Hạnh speaks of being able to have two roots—that is, having your spiritual ancestors in two traditions: "on the altar in my hermitage in France, I have statues of

---

13. Bidwell, *When One Religion*, 113.
14. Du Bois, "Strivings of the Negro People."

Buddhas and bodhisattvas and also an image of Jesus Christ. I do not feel any conflict within me. Instead, I feel stronger because I have more than one root."[15] For him, the two roots are Buddhism and Christianity. Nhất Hạnh knows the extraordinary value of dialogue and its ability to transform who you are—your identity and sense of self. "When you touch someone who authentically represents a tradition, you not only touch his or her tradition, you also touch your own. This quality is essential for dialogue. When participants are willing to learn from each other, dialogue takes place just by their being together."[16] Authenticity and interfaith exchange are an ongoing reality in many multicultural interfaith couples. Imagine the ways in which these partners lives are deepened from such ongoing long-term relationships. Spiritually fluid people and couples are like trees with more than one root, drawing strength and stability from more than one religious tradition, or, one might say, drinking in nourishment from multiple streams of life-giving water. As such, the fruits from the tree of our lives are sweeter and more complex.[17]

The fruits of double belonging include people who demonstrate gifted leadership, global perspectives, and insightful analytical abilities. "Research suggests that people who embody other types of multiplicity . . . think in more creative, flexible, and open-minded ways than does the general

---

15. Hạnh, *Living Buddha, Living Christ*, 100.

16. Hạnh, *Living Buddha, Living Christ*, 6–7.

17. Double belonging for clergy and leaders who live within an interfaith family is made even more complicated because of concerns for ordination, continued standing, and passing on the tenets of the religious tradition and the *orthodoxy and orthopraxy* within that tradition. My ordination was stalled by gatekeepers who adhered to a replacement model of theologies of religions, understanding that my role was to *convert others* to Christianity. The fact that my husband was Hindu was a sign that I was insufficient as a Christian leader. For myself, the concept of *double consciousness* can be demonstrated by the creation of two Facebook identities. As a spiritually fluid public theologian and minister, I needed these two separate social media spaces to manage these two distinct identities and worlds I moved between. One was for my professional life, where no reference to my Indian friends or Hindu festivals would be mentioned, and the other for my personal page, where family life was more open and transparent, including celebrations of Deepavali—the Hindu festival of lights. Questions of my legitimacy as a Christian leader can come up at any time from any sector within or outside of my congregation. In a very real way, my husband and our interfaith family have been a threat to the legitimacy of my leadership. This is something I have had to guard against for years. Only recently have I been able to integrate these two conscious ways of being into a more unified person and leader, in no small part related to my own success and legitimacy as a progressive pastor and resituating my credentials inside of the United Church of Christ. This book is a step toward claiming the truth that the gifts of double belonging far out-weigh the risks.

population," and "they demonstrate *generative imagination*, a creative turn serving the world in ways that care for, and improve the lives of, others."[18] As cross-cultural theological translators, spiritual advisors, or academic trail blazers, we can see that spiritual fluidity and double belonging are qualities that we may wish to seek out for leadership in a complex world that is plagued by clashing religious fundamentalists, political ideologues, and violent extremists. To paraphrase Fredrick Buechner, when the world's deepest needs meet the individual's greatest gifts, we say that it is our *calling*. My own journey as a person who belongs to two religious traditions, Hindu and Christian, and as a leader who advocates for, on behalf of, and alongside the poor in my church community, the call to a liberation theology of religions is truly "a calling, a compulsion, a necessity, a survival, a means to being whole."[19] Multicultural interfaith families not only belong here in our communities; they have remarkable stories to tell and extraordinary skills to share with the world.

18. Bidwell, *When One Religion*, 138–9.
19. Bidwell, *When One Religion*, 100.

9

Standing Up for Love

TELLING THE PARENTS

Shiva was twenty-five years old when he told his parents about his relationship with *this western woman*. His parents were in shock and disbelief, and they looked for an explanation for *how this could have happened*? Colleen understands the cultural differences between the Western worldview and the South Asian worldview. She explains, "I learned that he was very close with his family. They were family-centric and considered each other in decisions. When I looked at my family, which was divorced, people were very individualistic and, at times, narcissistic and self-serving. There was a lot of dysfunction. People were doing their own thing for themselves." She found this family-centric way of relating very attractive compared to the individualistic approach often advocated for within American households. While she was understanding and interested in these same shared values, she was about to become the focus of his parents' ire and blame. The conflict was only just beginning. Shiva explains what his parents were thinking at the time he talked to them, "'He is not in a right mind to make this decision. Maybe it's demons. There's a bad influence, negative influence. It's either her or something else' in my life. It is a bad period for me, astrologically, that they need to do something to fix it." He was too young to make decisions like this on his own, according to his parents. *She* must be the negative influence in his life, and they needed her to be removed—even *excised* from his life. They went to great lengths to save their son from Colleen.

With three of the couples I interviewed, this concept of the Hindu partner *choosing* their own marriage partner went against the cultural values of their respective families. When sharing the news of Usha's desire to marry Patrick, according to Usha, her mother said explicitly, "But I don't know this person: he's white, he's American he's non-veg." The whole list started coming out. "And more so, *I didn't get to choose*," said her mother. Notice the emphasis on the mother's understanding that it was her role to *choose* her daughter's marriage partner. Later in the same conversation, Usha's mother said, "But I'm not ready to get married." Meaning, she was not ready for *her daughter to get married*, nor was she ready to assume her role in preparing for and planning that wedding, which customarily fell upon the parents of the bride and groom.

A. S., from a Gujarati family, faced similar challenges of going against his families' cultural norms of arranged marriages when he decided to marry Máire, a white American-born Catholic woman. In his words, "So, ultimately, I said, 'Well, I'm in love with this person. So, we're gonna have to defy some of those cultural norms.'" The cultural norms A. S. speaks of are the traditional expectations within the Gujarati Hindu community of parents arranging the marriage of their children among eligible young men and women who fit the profile of the family—from earnings to looks, age, caste, and citizen status—all are matters that are disclosed in the resume profiles shared between families. Each eligible marriage candidate puts together a profile with bio data, education, work status and earnings. Then those are sent out and shared among members of their community in search for a suitable boy or girl for their adult child. A. S., who belongs to a tight-knit Gujarati community in the southern part of the United States, would be defying these norms by choosing for himself who to marry and, most especially, by marrying outside of the Indian community all together.

Each of the three families I interviewed comes from a different context in India—one is from a Rajasthani family, another from a Gujarati family, and our third couple is from a Tamil family. They are from three different states in India, they do not share caste identity or even religious orthodoxy. What they have in common is their Indian Hindu identity and the cultural practice of arranging marriages for their children. Two families moved to the United States from India as young adults. Yet Usha was born on the East Coast of the United States. Whether citizens of the US or not, Shiva, Usha, and A. S. are still tightly connected to their Indian families' cultural heritage and practices. The tension between choosing to marry your own partner or allowing the cultural practice of arranged marriages to continue highlights competing value systems. Which values are more important, the individual right to choose or the community's need to retain its cultural distinctiveness? Within the community, cultural and religious preservation is based, in part, by the successful passing on of traditional food and recipes, regional language, religious and ethnic practices to the next generation, and that, it can be argued, is best accomplished by marrying within the same community. Yet living within a particular community and adhering to traditional practices may compete with what is best for the individual when whom they love is among those who are considered off-limits, outsiders, or even outlawed in their religious communities. For instance, within some states in India, marriage between Hindus and Muslims are considered forced marriages and are, in fact, outlawed.[1] With the rise of the Hindu party, the BJP, states in India have enacted tougher laws that prevent young couples from getting married. Their desired marriage to a community outsider is considered problematic. Families will go to great lengths to try to break these relationships up. An organization has emerged to try to help these couples. "To counter the hate and bigotry directed at interfaith couples, married couple Samar Halarnkar and Priya Ramani launched the 'India Love Project' on Instagram in 2020, which rejects religious polarization and celebrates interfaith relationships."[2] The rights of the individual to choose who they will marry for themselves arises from Western values and is impacting generations of families with the Indian context and the Indian diaspora. The Indian culture prioritizes family, community connections, and preserving the traditions and religious practices within their subcommunity. These values, including arranged marriages within their family's religious community, are there, it is believed, for the benefit of the couple, their compatibility, and longevity of the marriage.

Some couples choose to retain parts of their culture, others choose to eschew it altogether. For my husband, Sriram, he desired to leave behind the aspects of his culture that he found burdensome. When he stood up for our marriage against the resistance of his parents, he was also standing up for his own values. He despised the levels of corruption and bribery required in everyday life in Bombay that he experienced growing up there in the 1980s. He appreciated the reliability of the American infrastructure—there were neither power cuts of electricity nor water rations for cooking and bathing in

1. See, for instance, Frayer, "New Law in India."
2. Krishnan, "Why Interfaith Marriage."

the Midwest United States. Choosing to marry someone from the Western cultural value system aligned with his own values. For my part, I always felt guilty that I was keeping him from returning to his homeland. I wondered if he would ever regret marrying me versus having married a beautiful black-haired Indian Hindu Iyengar woman. I worried that he would have been happier with someone from his own religious and cultural community. If he had done it the "right way," maybe he would have been happier. But then we encountered young couples within his own family who followed all the traditional arranged marriage practices, and they divorced early in their relationship. The "right way" did not work for them either. Times were changing within his own family. I stopped worrying about us doing it the "wrong way" so much after that. Occasionally we would discuss the option of moving back to India, but he was never seriously interested, not just because of me, but because his sense of self and identity had changed as well. He found his belonging in the United States and with a white American-born Christian woman. Yet there are always benefits and costs to these kinds of decisions.

Maria and Adam, our Catholic/Jewish couple living in Costa Rica, faced institutional resistance from both of their religious communities—Maria met resistance within her Costa Rican Catholic Church, and Adam faced resistance with his Reform Jewish synagogue in North Carolina. When they sought out doctors who would be willing to circumcise their son according to Jewish custom, they experienced institutional resistance from the local medical community. They discovered that circumcision is not practiced in Costa Rica. It took many phone calls and conversations with a variety of medical and religious professionals before they were able to secure a doctor who was trained and willing to perform the medical procedure on their little boy. A *mohel*, a Jewish professional specially trained to perform circumcisions, was very difficult to come by. Adam was told once by another Jewish family not to use the *mohel* they used for their son; *they would not recommend him for another family*. Eventually they did find a local doctor to perform the procedure, but it was not a religious *bris*. Later, when they visited Adam's hometown in the United States, they found a progressive rabbi, a woman, who performed an adapted ceremony focusing on the opening of their son's senses based, in part, on suggestions found in Miller's book.[3]

The most difficult aspect of sharing his relationship occurred when Adam went to talk to his own religious clergy about Maria. When he

---

3. Miller, *Being Both*, 132.

approached his rabbi in the United States to share the news of his relationship, Adam became upset. He shares how he felt during that encounter:

> It's really disheartening for me. When, before Maria [and I] even got engaged, I was doing a lot of outreach to my rabbi back in [the city], where I grew up going to that congregation in the reform tradition. I reached out to a reconstructionist synagogue and no one was supportive. And, for me, it was really difficult because it was the first time that I really felt excluded from a group. 'Cause I had been active at the temple and active in Hillel on campus. And so, I felt, as soon as I was making the statement about yes, you know, I'm marrying someone who's not Jewish, and, yes, I'm going to have kids that are raised in both. I felt immediately, sort of, pushed out.

These conversations played a central role in his own interfaith identity formation. He had not imagined that he would be unwelcome in his reformed Jewish religious community, nor that the woman he loved would not be welcomed within his reformed synagogue. It was surprising and unsettling. He encountered the reality that many multicultural interfaith couples face, *you are asked to choose one religious tradition over another if you want to remain a part of your home religious community.* This is particularly painful. The only alternative may seem to be to let go of your religious identity, because letting go of who you love is not an option. Letting go of their religious connections is what happened to Adam's parents and what contributed to their own cultural practice of Judaism. Adam believed that he and Maria would not be able to have a religious ceremony, so he resigned himself to having a civil ceremony based on his own parents' experience.

> My dad is Jewish, my mom's not practicing, but she was raised Catholic. When they were getting married in the late eighties, they were trying to find a rabbi, in the city where I'm from, that would marry them. No rabbi would do it. So, they were like, okay, we'll just have a civil wedding. And so, to me, I almost preferred it because I thought, well, it's the most neutral.

In the end, they were able to find support from Maria's priest; though, initially, she was afraid that no priest would marry them because they were from different religions. Maria could not imagine a nonreligious ceremony. She explains, "Well, for me, it was very important to get married in the Catholic church. A civil wedding wasn't an option for me." In a dramatic gesture of welcome and inclusion, their Catholic priest offered to incorporate Adam's Jewish *tallit* into the ceremony. The *tallit* is a special Jewish prayer shawl that is often presented and first worn at a child's coming-of-age ceremony—at their *bat mitzvah* or *bar mitzvah*. Adam tells of the moment in the ceremony, "He wrapped the tallit around us for the wedding. My parents had already arrived for the wedding. When I told my parents, my dad started crying. This was just really was touching to him."[4] They were able to incorporate the *tallit* that was made for him by his aunt and presented to him at his *bar mitzvah*. This moment is a cherished photo of the couple from their wedding and a sign of their interfaith marriage. Maria stood up for their relationship and, subsequently, her priest made it possible for Adam's religious expression to be included in the wedding ceremony. These acts of inclusion by clergy, who have the power to bless or shun, are profoundly healing for the couple and the extended family.

One of the greatest forces for good or for harm in the life of a newly engaged multicultural interfaith couple is their local faith community and its clergy leadership. Local priests, rabbis, ministers, and imams have the power to bless or the power to exclude couples who present relationships that cross identified barriers of acceptability as suitable marriage partners. Paul and Cathy, married for over forty years, are peace activists and a spiritually fluid couple. Paul and Cathy, our Buddhist-Catholic/Buddhist couple, faced institutional obstacles and resistance when they chose to have a sacramental wedding within the Catholic church. To do so meant that Cathy's previous divorce had to be formally annulled within the church. Cathy faced intensely personal questions and scrutiny not only from their local priest but also from their bishop. Once they learned the annulment was approved, they set their wedding date. Surprisingly, they were then informed that before the annulment would be finalized their request had to go before a tribunal for review. Cathy recalls, "It wasn't a pleasant process, meeting with the Jesuit priest. He had questions that he had to ask me. Lots of very personal and intimate questions." The fact that she was wrestling with internal questions regarding the institutional church's sexist language and patriarchal practices made this endeavor more troubling. Paul, a Catholic theologian working within a Catholic University, to maintain his own professional credibility, wanted their marriage to be within the church. "As a Catholic, I wanted the marriage to be sacramental. Politically, if I wanted to keep my job I couldn't be married [to Cathy without the annulment]. I

---

4. See Appendix A for a photo of Maria and Adam with the tallit wrapped around them during the marriage ceremony.

couldn't be 'living in sin' according to the Catholic church and not be validly married." The annulment was the only way that could happen. As the date for their wedding drew closer, the stress was mounting as to whether or not the tribunal was going to rule in favor of the annulment. They turned to their local priest as an ally. Cathy explains, "This Jesuit that I worked with really challenged the archdiocese and the tribunal. He really pushed them. So, we did get [the annulment] in time."

Paul was facing pressures of his own within his workplace because of his theological views toward other religious traditions; his colleagues "would have been very happy to see me go," Paul remembers. He found out later that it was important professionally that his marriage was *within the Catholic church*, indicating it could have been another bit of evidence to discredit his Christology. "I was investigated by the Congregation for the Doctrine of the Faith, and the Bishop in Cincinnati got letters from Cardinal Ratzinger, at the time, telling him that I should be fired. That was because of my Christology—questioning Jesus as the one and only Savior. It's a pluralistic Christology. Had I been married 'outside the church,' as they put it, I would not have been in good standing as a Catholic theologian." The institutional resistance to their marriage was more than a matter of personal faith; it was a matter of religious doctrine and professional legitimacy. While most couples will not likely face this level of institutional resistance, many do face questions of their religious identity—for instance, it is not uncommon to hear that your religious credentials are weakened because of who you married. *You aren't a real Jew if your partner isn't also Jewish. You can't be Christian and be married to a someone who is Hindu.* In my case, my ordination process faced obstacles, both within the Presbyterian Church (USA) (a.k.a. PCUSA) and the Christian Church (Disciples of Christ). Ordination committees in both of these denominations questioned my legitimate claim to be called to Christian ministry because I had not *converted my husband from Hinduism to Christianity.* Interfaith couples, like Paul and Cathy, must learn skills of negotiation and adaptation, and develop strong allies to support them against generations of policies and doctrines designed to uphold exclusionary practices and the traditional power of religious institutions.

10

Remaking Rituals

THE PRACTICE OF RELIGIOUS rituals and cultural practices within multicultural interfaith couples requires a closer look at the embedded values toward religious others that may not be obvious to those inside the religious tradition. But to the *religiously othered* partner those statements of faith, liturgies or clothing practices may make them feel unwelcome or excluded in unintentional ways. The details of these rituals will often be discussed at length between the couples and with their families and religious leaders to ensure that they represent the shared inclusive values of this newly forming family. Some practices are traditionally gendered for boys only, such as the Hindu thread ceremony or the Jewish bris. Other practices may make assumptions about the families' unified beliefs in one religious tradition, such as the liturgy for baptism of infants in the Christian tradition, which asks that the parents reaffirm their faith and belief in Jesus as the Christ. One of the opportunities that these couples have is to remake these rituals in ways that honor both parents' cultures and religions. These rites of passage also give the multicultural interfaith couple a chance to share the new values with their religious leaders and work in partnership to fashion inclusive and pluralistic rituals that honor the reality of the changing landscape of multicultural marriages and interfaith families. This is one of the blessings that interfaith couples bring to our religious communities—they analyze and remake rituals to fit the changing cultural times we live within.

When their relationship was forming, Usha and Patrick took the time they needed to receive the blessing and support from both sides of their families for their two traditional religious wedding ceremonies. They were married by two priests—first by a Hindu priest in India, then, after their return, by a Catholic priest in the United States. They held a traditional Hindu Rajasthani wedding in India, where Patrick wore traditional Indian wedding attire, including a turban; with members of family alongside, he made a grand entrance into the wedding by riding in on a horse. During that ceremony the elders conducted a ritual usually reserved for Brahmin men. Patrick shares, "I don't know what would count as conversion to Hinduism. It is true that I had to undergo a ceremony that invested me with the thread. And I had to recite the Gayatri-mantra and that was about it. And they were like, okay, you're all set." This rite of passage is normally conducted for young boys or young men from Brahmin families. That they conducted a ceremony like this shows that Usha's family desired to welcome Patrick fully into their community. Usha spoke of her father's brother, who took a leadership role in supporting Patrick during this aspect of the wedding. "My uncle sponsored him through that. One of my paternal uncles decided to sponsor Patrick as officially adopted. My uncle has only four sons, so he's like, okay, I'll take the fifth. We jokingly called my aunt, after that, the Pandavas' mother." This reference to the "Pandavas" evokes one of the sacred stories of Hinduism about five sons who are the main heroic characters of the Hindu epic the *Mahabharatha*. It is a religious tale of good versus evil, an exploration of just wars and ethical behavior in the face of envy, greed, and temptation. The story of the Pandavas, the five brothers, forms the backdrop for the story of Lord Krishna in the *Bhagavad Gita*—which is literally translated as the "divine song." Usha's paternal uncle "adopting" Patrick, and claiming him as one of the Pandavas of his family, suggests inclusion and religious welcome at the highest level for such a multicultural interfaith couple.

These entirely new blended rituals fuse diverse families and values together in beautiful ways where both sides feel included and valued. Moreover, the children of these multicultural couples learn that they belong to both of their parents' religious and cultural identities during the performance of these religious rites. Another blessing is the inclusion of the *religiously othered* extended family members in these gatherings. For example, when the *tallit* from the Jewish ritual of *bar mitzvas* for boys is allowed by the minister to be worn during a Christian confirmation process for a Jewish-Christian child, both families of faith can feel that their blessings are resting upon the child, not one or the other tradition is given precedence over the other. The child is celebrated. In some cases, these rituals were only reserved for members of that particular faith. When the multicultural interfaith family negotiates these expectations with their clergy partners, they expand who is welcome and what is considered normal within their faith community. There is a mutually beneficial expansion of beliefs and practices that can follow from the innovative work these couples bring to their religious communities.

Another example of movement toward inclusion in these traditional families happened when Kamran's Muslim family came to Kamalpreet's Sikh household and formally asked her parents for her hand in marriage. Kamran talks of his mother's transformation prior to going to the home of his fiancée's parents: "My mom has become surprisingly open. I kind of tried to rationalize things to my mom. 'I know it's not the same religion. But the fundamental beliefs are the same fundamental meaning. They're both monotheistic religions.'" This *preengagement* ceremony is based on the Indian cultural concept of a *rokha*, which means "stop," referring to the practice of arranging marriages. A *rokha* is performed when the families agree to stop receiving prospective matches for their son or daughter. Kamalpreet smiles as she tells of all who were there for the ceremony, "It was Kamran's brother and his mom and dad. And then on my side, it was me, my mom and dad, my brother, my two cousins and my aunt and uncle, who live next door. It wasn't like a formal event. It was more like, 'Hey, we accept you guys. You guys can now move on to the next step.' They basically gave us their blessings."

Kamalpreet's family is more culturally Sikh than religiously Sikh—meaning they will participate in holidays and other functions, but they do not attend the *Gurudwara* regularly, nor do they wear the symbols of their faith. Both Kamran and Kamalpreet showed skills of patience and perseverance in the face of issues that cross national and religious identities. What they have discovered over these years of dating and working through their familial differences is while there is conflict between their religious and national identities, there is a common cultural heritage based in South Asian traditions that are not tied to any one nation or religion. This has helped Kamran and Kamalpreet bridge the differences between their families as they point out the shared cultural similarities—they share similar languages, as Urdu and Punjabi are linguistically connected; they share similar marriage practices, such as the *rokha*; and they emphasize that they both belong to monotheistic faith traditions.

Multicultural interfaith couples often learn the skills of patience and perseverance out of their deep love for one another and respect for their partner's family. It takes time to learn about the complex details of traditional ceremonies, then to navigate with clergy leaders, to negotiate with their partner, and to then develop new rituals for their blended family. These skills often begin to form in the planning stages of the wedding—or weddings, if they want to celebrate both religious ceremonies. These adaptive skills are useful beyond the wedding. Opportunities for merging their diverse lives will occur at each life stage of their relationship and growing family.

Colleen and Shiva took the time to invent their own coming-of-age rite of passage for their son, eschewing the traditional South Indian thread ceremony ritual, customarily performed for Brahmin boys. Instead, they planned an overnight travel weekend for their son, accompanied by his uncles and father. While doing that, they had to continue their advocacy for people who are LGBTQ because Colleen's older brother is gay and is in a committed relationship. Shiva has a younger brother who lives in the United States. He was raised in the same traditional Tamil household that would not normally be accepting of other expressions of sexuality. His brother would have been uncomfortable with attending an event with Colleen's brother and his partner present. While planning for this special rite of passage for their son, Shiva explained to his brother that they wanted both of his uncles present, and they had invited Colleen's brother's partner as well. Should Shiva's brother feel that he could not attend because Colleen's brother and his partner would be present, while they would be disappointed, they would understand. Shiva's brother decided after that conversation that he would attend the overnight event with his nephew. Perhaps, for the first time, Shiva's brother had his eyes opened to a loving gay relationship. That is a remarkable shift toward cultural inclusiveness in just a few short years.

11

The History of Us versus Them

MULTICULTURAL INTERFAITH COUPLES FACE conflict and tensions that are complex and nuanced. Their personal stories are interwoven into larger national conversations, political movements, and changing religious doctrines. The couples I interviewed often found themselves caught in the middle of a larger conflict beyond their control. They could be caught between two religions with a history of conflict and war; squeezed by religious institutional practices that forbid marriage if they are divorced or from a different religion; or impacted by shifting governmental border politics as their home country's borders are being redrawn. Love happens across national borders. Love happens across religious traditions. Love happens across cultural divides. Love happens across racial communities. The personal experiences of multicultural interfaith couples can reflect the national realities of political and religious conflict. As cultural tensions rise, so may the challenges these couples encounter in their everyday life. Microaggressions, racist rhetoric, and threats of violence against one or both members of the couple can increase as the cultural climate in their communities becomes less welcoming of people of color, people of othered religious traditions, or as immigration policies become platforms for inciting fear of the stranger. With each of the couples I interviewed, conversations about religion, race, culture, and national identity within their own lives mirrored national conversations. Some even referred to national moments or *flashpoints* in history that reflected their personal reality.

A flashpoint is the lowest temperature at which a gaseous substance can spontaneously combust—or burst into flames. At the flashpoint temperature, that substance may not only ignite but may also explode without any additional spark. If not handled properly, gasoline fumes, for instance, can spontaneously explode. Another way to look at tension and conflict in multicultural interfaith relationships is this: a match striking against a friction surface creates tension and sparks, which then ignite the fuel on the end of the wooden match. That burning flame, then, is used to start a bigger fire. But what if you do not need the match at all? The fuel is there waiting for the right conditions, a flashpoint incident, which then sets the fire ablaze. We live in a world where there are smoldering conflicts lying just below the surface. *When someone challenges the way things are done in a traditional family, that friction can set off a chain reaction and turn into something larger very quickly.* These flashpoint incidents can be personal—when you bring home the person you love and want to marry to meet your parents. The flashpoints can impact the lives of an entire nation and turn political—for instance a country's sudden policy shift on immigration.

This metaphor of flashpoints can help us understand the complexities of living at the intersections of multiple identities that create othered lives. Further, a person's ability to successfully navigate these overlapping forms of discrimination that cross nationality, race, culture, and religion in their personal circumstances, makes multicultural interfaith couples ideal leaders and social change agents in their communities. These flashpoints remind us that the conflicts these couples face are often microcosms of larger tensions occurring nationally or globally. In the pages ahead we will explore interfaith marriages in the section "When Religion Matters," and the national flashpoint in India of the "Babri Masjid Incident"; we will deepen our appreciation of interracial relationships in the section "When Race Matters," and the United States national flashpoint of the "George Floyd Incident"; we will enter into the complexities of culture wars and competing worldviews of cross-cultural relationships in "When Culture Matters," and the flashpoint of the "US Capitol Insurgency Incident"; and, finally, with the flashpoint of the "Muslim Ban Incident," we will attempt to grasp the indivisibility of nationality, religion, and culture in the section "When National Identity and Border Politics Matter."

"Fault line wars," as described by Samuel Huntington in *The Clash of Civilizations*, "are off-again-on-again wars that can flame up into massive violence and then sputter down into low-intensity warfare of sullen hostility only to flame up once again. The fires of communal identity and hatred are rarely totally extinguished."[1] These wars between people of different religions are ultimately "rooted in the identities of people,"[2] where much is at stake. When people from different cultures, races, and religions come together, whose traditions cross these "fault lines," the simmering undercurrents of fear, hatred, misunderstanding, and prejudicial stereotypes rise to the surface as families try to prevent *what should not be* from happening. Hindus *should not marry* Christians; Sikhs *should not marry* Muslims; Catholics *should not marry* Jews. These are not just family preferences; these are long-standing generational conflicts that rise and fall and are tied to former wars and conflicts where many people died, often in the name of *religion*. When my then boyfriend called his parents, whether in the forefront of their minds or not, they were confronting years of Christian supremacy and Britain's colonial rule of India for over two hundred years. Their worst fears were coming true—their firstborn son was intending to marry outside of their caste and religion. When young couples share the news of their love with their parents, this can become a flashpoint for religious conflicts, identity politics, culture wars, or racial tensions. What seems like a matter between two people suddenly becomes a matter crossing borders, faith, and generations of tradition. What lessons can we learn from these couples who dared to love across these fault lines of faith and culture?

WHEN RELIGION MATTERS

We are living in a time in American history when the fastest growing religious group is people who have no religious affiliation—often referred to as "nones,"[3] that is, people who do not claim to belong or affiliate with any religious tradition. "One-fifth of the U.S. public—and a third of adults under the age of 30—are religiously unaffiliated today, the highest percentages ever in the Pew Research Center polling."[4] It could be argued that religion matters less today than in years past. Perhaps, while more people, especially younger generations, are less religious than their parents, to neglect the role that religion and religious values play in our everyday lives may cause us to miss some essential gifts that multicultural interfaith couples have to share with the world. In short, religion still matters a great deal. I believe religion

1. Huntington, *Clash of Civilizations*, 253.
2. Huntington, *Clash of Civilizations*, 253.
3. Pew Research Center, "'Nones' on the Rise."
4. Pew Research Center, "'Nones' on the Rise."

matters, not only in shaping our values and faith but it contains insights for solving complex cultural problems. When we practice committed long-term interfaith religious engagement, like many multicultural interfaith couples do, it may unlock avenues of peace and methods of collaboration that we need in the ever-increasing conflictual global tensions of our times.

Flashpoint: The Babri Masjid Incident

Usha was studying her final year of college in the United States when Hindu nationals, in 1992, demolished a historic Islamic Mosque in Ayodhya, on top of what is believed to be the birthplace of Lord Ram of the Hindu religion. American-born Usha, from an upper caste, is a daughter of a Brahmin family, whose ancestors served in the court of kings in north India. She began learning Persian in college on the East Coast so that she could read, for herself, the documents from the sixteenth-century Mughal period, when the mosque was originally built. There has been a long-standing religious dispute between Muslims and Hindus over ownership of the site. After an earlier lower court ruling divided the site between the Muslims and the Hindus, the case was sent onward to be heard by the Indian Supreme Court. In a landmark ruling, India's Supreme Court granted full rights of the disputed site to Hindus. On the physical site where the ancient mosque once stood, construction is now finished on what is being called "a Hindu Vatican City."[5] The "Babri Masjid" incident was a flashpoint between Hindus and Muslims in northern India. The riots after the demolition incident in 1992 resulted in over two thousand deaths.[6] The Babri Masjid incident took place in the region of India where Usha's family is from and is of personal importance to Usha and Patrick.

Usha and Patrick are a UU-Hindu/Catholic-Christian couple living in the Midwest. For Usha, studying Persian was a matter of "trying to figure out what my heritage is, what my origins are, what makes sense, and what doesn't make sense." Married to an American Catholic-Christian, her questions of identity center around her religious and national identities. She continues, "[I had] a deep knowing that in the late eighties and the early nineties, the Mughal period was being talked about both in South Asia and in India, in particular with all the brewing up of the Babri Masjid, that something was deeply, deeply wrong. In the same way that we know that

5. Nair et al., "Ayodhya."
6. Tully, "How the Babri Mosque."

there's something deeply, deeply wrong in our country right now." She is referring here to the presidency of Donald Trump and the culture wars stoked by the lead-up to the 2020 presidential election.

Together Patrick and Usha have taken students to India on two occasions for three-week educational, immersive, cross-cultural experiences. And most recently, Usha and Patrick sponsored more than thirty students during their "study away" program, where, together, their family and the students all lived in England during the students' junior year at the university. Through their university they have invited undergraduate students into their home for cultural experiences, such as shared meals and celebrations of Hindu holidays. Usha has been invited to host chapel services, where, over the years, she has gone from offering talks about Diwali and Hinduism to being allowed to invite students to *participate in religious rituals*, like holding a *diya*, a little oil lamp, and offering light to one of the Hindu deities for Diwali. She has garnered trust within this small Christian University, and helped them move into a deeper appreciation of other world religions.

Usha and Patrick, both educated in the history of South Asia, especially the Mughal period, have shared their personal experiences of their complex multicultural interfaith family with their students. They are ambassadors for interfaith exchanges and dialogue. They understand the importance of cross-cultural and religious experiences in the lives of students who have had little to no exposure outside of their mostly white midwestern Christian home communities.

Religious exchanges, interfaith dialogue, and immersive experiences are all a part of this unique couple's social change agency within their community. When asked about their religious affiliation and if they consider themselves Catholic, Christian, Hindu, or Unitarian Universalists, their response is more nuanced. "We are officially members of both the Catholic church and the Lutheran church. Because the Lutheran church allows us to be members of their church without being Lutheran and we are also friends of the local U. U." They are a spiritually fluid family participating in a variety of religious communities and exposing their young sons, as much as they are able, to these diverse experiences. Like other kids, their favorite part of church is always the cookies. Describing her family, Usha simply states, "We are interfaith people."

WHEN RACE MATTERS

My mother lived and worked in Selma, Alabama, in the 1960s. She came from a poor, lower-class white family—both her parents were conservative Christian ministers. She married early, did not graduate from high school, and soon found herself divorced with four children. As an uneducated divorcée with four young children living in a racially divided city during the Civil Rights Movement, she understood what it meant to be an outcast. Survival is all that mattered. She had to navigate race and poverty in a politically and racially charged atmosphere. The country's eyes were on Selma, especially in March of 1965, during the Selma to Montgomery march to the statehouse. Her teenage daughter, my elder sister, was on the sidelines hurling words one should not say towards the Black marchers that day. When my mother married my father a month later, my granddaddy told her, as she headed up to Ohio (which would become my birthplace), not to talk about race, politics, or religion *up North*. And she did not. Thus, matters of race and white privilege went underground, and I was beset with a blindness that would not be lifted until fifty years later, in 2015, while sitting at a lunch table with other colleagues marking the anniversary of that same Selma to Montgomery march.

In the heart of downtown Chicago, the Chicago Theological Seminary invited clergy and activists to a conference celebrating "Selma at 50." After the morning plenary session, I joined three Black clergy for lunch and conversation. I shared about my mother's experiences in Selma and then talked about my own interfaith family. (At the time, our two children were both in high school.) They seemed interested in learning more about our kids and my Indian Hindu husband. One clergyman with an especially dark complexion asked me if my kids thought of themselves as biracial. I said, "I don't think so." He encouraged me to go home and ask them the question and then listen for their answer. I did. I was surprised that not only did they think of themselves as "biracial," they could speak freely about it. Why couldn't I see our family as biracial? Had I inherited my family's self-imposed blindness? Perhaps Granddaddy's charge to my mother to remain silent to ensure her safety contributed to my own subsequent lack of vision. I returned the next day to the conference and had lunch with the same three people. Amazed that I did not realize this before, the two clergywomen with me asked, "How could this be?" The Black clergyman took my white hand in his, rubbed my skin, smiled, and said, "Because of this." From then onward, I began to notice race and talk about privilege in my own family. Race became a matter to contend with in the open.

Flashpoint: The George Floyd Incident

Our country experienced a national wake-up call on May 25, 2020. Video footage released on social media showed Minneapolis resident George Floyd calling out to his mother and crying, "I can't breathe," as white officer Derek Chauvin kneeled on his neck for eight minutes and forty-six seconds, suffocating him to death. *I can't breathe* was etched in the memory of many as we recalled the highly publicized death of Eric Garner in the summer of 2015 in New York. Floyd's cry echoed Garner's and turned into a national rallying cry for the Black Lives Matter movement. People began chanting, "I can't breathe! I can't breathe! Eight minutes and forty-six seconds!" This is our flashpoint around race. Spontaneous rallies, protests, and marches erupted across the country as part of the Black Lives Matter movement with calls to defund the police and put an end to police violence against people of color. The movement brought attention to the long-standing discriminatory practices against people of color. It reached across the racial divides and into the homes of privileged white suburban communities, highlighting the disproportionate responses that white people receive during routine traffic stops versus people of color, who have, for years, been dealing with brutality and violence, especially from white police officers. The summer of 2020 could be considered a *metanoia* event for our country—an eye-opening, identity-transforming national awakening. As we are waking up to the impact that race and class has on people of color within the United States, our next interviewed couple experiences their own wake-up call to white privilege and the impact that racism and poverty play in their own lives.

Couples and Race

When marriages cross racial and religious boundaries, one category may outweigh the other. My husband's skin color is not *that dark*, so racial tensions were not high enough in my experience for me to explicitly take notice until that meeting at the lunch table. Afterwards, I began to recall when we *pass* and when we *do not pass for white* in white spaces or when we pass or do not pass for Indian in Indian spaces. We live in both worlds but do not fully belong in either. For some of the couples I interviewed, racial blindness is not an option. They are reminded by the people and the spaces they occupy. For them race matters a great deal.

Attending a racially diverse university in the South was an eye-opener for Máire. There she met A. S., who originally immigrated from Gujarat, India, to Los Angeles with his parents when he was seven years old. They soon became college freshman sweethearts—but kept their relationship to themselves and among their friends. A. S., raised in a Hindu community, is a self-described atheist. In a family with two young sons, he supports Máire in raising their children in the church. They celebrate Hindu holidays, such as Diwali, and had two weddings—one Catholic and one Hindu. When asked about experiences of discrimination or racial incidents, A. S. shares that when he first came to America he remembers waking up as a young child to gun fire in his neighborhood after the Rodney King trial verdict. "It was odd because we moved—and we were relatively well off in India. Then we moved and we were in the middle of gunshots being fired there. You could hear blasts in the middle of the night. As a child, you're wondering, 'What kind of third world country did I move to?'" His father had a master's degree in chemistry from India, but, after immigrating here, he could not find work in his field. He became an hourly laborer in a warehouse. A. S.'s family went from middle-class in India to among the working poor in America. The housing they could afford placed them among the urban poor in Los Angeles until they landed in the urban South. You might say that A. S. woke up brown and poor in America. The intersection of race and poverty impacted his family directly—where he could live, where he went to school; ultimately, it shaped his sense of self in the world. He describes this journey of finding an American identity, "Finding my place in American culture, how do I define [myself] as a person, [as a] first generation? How do I see myself fitting into this society?"

Many of the multicultural interfaith couples I interviewed expressed similar views of experiencing a changing sense of self as they navigated their relationship with someone who did not share their family's culture, religion, class, or race. For A. S. and Máire, the early part of their relationship was a time of great learning to understand their divergent family backgrounds and contexts. For Máire, meeting A. S. was truly a life-changing experience. Máire, a self-described naïve young woman, was not aware of race or racist symbols, such as the Confederate flag, until A. S. explained it to her. Her eyes were opened in the course of their relationship. One incident in particular shaped her understanding. In her husband's words, this is what happened:

> One of her great friends from high school was dating a girl from the rural South and we'd gone to their home. There was a Confederate flag and mammy dolls. They had [pictures] of African Americans eating watermelons. Her stepfather made some comment to the effect of, "Oh, what's a pretty girl like you doing with him?" And I knew exactly what he meant. And he said it again, subtly, "You know what I mean. He's very lucky to have you." I remember being in that situation [and thinking], "What is this moron talking about? I'm a college-educated individual who earns way more than he could imagine earning and I'm being talked to in this manner. Who are you to talk to me in this way?" My personal accomplishments are completely disregarded.

While A. S. could see the prejudicial racist remarks for what they were, Máire could not read the room or recognize the racial undertones of that interaction. Until A. S. later explained, Máire had thought the flag was just a symbol of the war, not an ongoing symbol of white supremacy and racial discrimination toward people of color. When A. S. shared his experiences of growing up in India and Los Angeles, Máire not only learned about the injustice and racial hatred that A. S. and his friends experienced, but she was also able to see the interlocking problems of race and poverty for herself.

> I didn't know until afterwards because I grew up in the North. I didn't understand what the Confederate flag meant until much later in my adult life. I had no real concept of the civil rights struggles. I had no concept that it stood for racism. I thought it just stood for the war, the South lost. So, I was naïve of a lot of the racist undertones. A. S. actually educated me on those examples. He went to underperforming, primarily African American schools because they lived in a very impoverished part of [the city]. It was back when they were still bussing. He was one of the kids that got bussed.

Her relationship provided her with insight she did not previously have. Her eyes were opened to matters of race and poverty. The challenges of immigration, poverty, and cultural differences that people of color face in their daily lives in the United States became important to Máire *because A. S. was important to her.* Her white privilege was undistinguished prior to her relationship with her husband. She experienced a personal transformation, a shift in her identity.

White Americans who marry darker-skinned partners may experience racial tension and conflict personally for the first time. When directed at the one they love, it opens their eyes to race in new ways. Their family may now live at the intersection of prejudice, microaggressions, and discrimination. Multicultural interfaith couples learn quickly how to navigate these new circumstances of prejudice often originating with their own families of origin, whom they also love dearly. One skill that can develop over time is compassion for those who have not had the experiences or education on racial challenges. When our grandparents question our choice in marriage partners, some of their comments can come from deeply racialized lives. Us versus them mentalities place this newcomer to the family firmly in the category of outsider.

For example, Colleen's grandmother's questions were centered more around their different racial backgrounds. "My grandmother's first question was, 'How dark is he?' I said, 'He's a beautiful brown. It's the color I've been trying to tan myself to all these years on the beach.' She did not find that humorous. She just looked at me." For Colleen's family then, racial and cultural differences were points of tension, but Colleen's family did little to prevent the marriage from moving forward. From the Western cultural perspective, of course, it was her choice to decide who she would marry.

In the end, Colleen and Shiva planned a mountainside wedding that combined ceremonial aspects from both of their traditions. They did not have a Hindu priest or a Christian minister present to preside over the wedding. Instead, they invited their friends, my husband and myself, to serve as facilitators of the short ceremony. Shiva's parents did not attend the ceremony and remained reticent against their relationship for some time. Yet, Shiva continued to visit his parents at their home in Tamil Nadu. Colleen rarely visited with him because she was not welcome.

Racial and cultural divides are hard to overcome. It may take years for those barriers to be torn down, if it happens at all. In some cases, these multicultural interfaith couples persevere in love with their prejudice families and judgmental in-laws. Over time those racial and cultural barriers may lower or fall away until what remains in its place is appreciation, acceptance, and love.[7] Our couple Colleen and Shiva eventually experienced acceptance and love from Shiva's parents. It was a joyous occasion when his

---

7. See photos of both ceremonies in Appendix A.

parents hosted a reenactment of the traditional Hindu wedding ceremony for their couple in honor of their son's fiftieth birthday.

WHEN CULTURE MATTERS

Matters of race, class, religion, and privilege are everyday concerns for multicultural interfaith couples given the kinds of tension and conflict they may go through in the formation of their relationship. In the process they may develop skills of navigating cultural spaces where questions of belonging can erupt into more than tension or arguments. Loving across cultures may cause long-lasting difficulties in families; divisions and rifts may linger or even fracture relationships.

Flashpoint: The US Capitol Insurgency Incident

The United States has been enmeshed in a culture war between Christian nationalism, centered in traditional American conservative white heteronormative values, and the more progressive, inclusive, and diverse community of Americans who value multiculturalism, racial equity, religious pluralism, queer rights, and gender equity. Former President Trump stoked the fires of these culture wars daily in his tweets and policies. Ultimately, the flashpoint for the culture wars in America occurred on January 6, 2021, on the day that the Senate and House were certifying the election results of President Elect Joe Biden. Trump refused to concede the election and encouraged thousands of protesters to march to the Capitol. Minutes later the protesters began to break through barriers and storm the Capitol in a violent raid, which resulted in five deaths. Carrying signs and symbols of Christian nationalism, they took over the Senate and House chambers and endangered the lives of our elected officials as the latter were hastily evacuated and found themselves cowering in undisclosed locations until the US Capitol was secured hours later. This collective experience of witnessing the Capitol insurrection, incited by our own president, was, perhaps, another wake-up call. Not only would the culture wars come into focus, but these deep cultural divides have caused real damage to our democracy and our communities. Perhaps it is time that we listen deeply across the chasm of cultural differences and discover new ways of connecting and relating to one another. The next multicultural interfaith couple spent years working across the cultures that separated them in order to gain the support and trust of their parents.

Couples and Culture

Our next couple learned how to persevere in the face on-going familial opposition. Colleen and Shiva, a UU-Buddhist married to an Indian Tamil Hindu, broke all the rules when they married more than twenty years ago. This is their story. Leaving the enclave of Hindu traditionalism in a coastal city in Tamil Nadu, a southern state in India, Shiva traveled to the United States for graduate school and attended a small engineering university in the Rocky Mountain region. There he met Colleen, who was living and working in the same city. She grew up in Florida, in an upper middle-class family, and attended a private university not far from home. Her parents were divorced while she was still in school. She had been previously married, but that marriage ended as quickly as it began. Nine years older than Shiva, Colleen was raised in a loosely Catholic household, but left that religious tradition many years ago. Now a self-described integral philosopher and spiritually fluid UU-Buddhist, she was intrigued with Shiva's Indian culture, values, and worldview. Shiva was naïve and curious himself, about Colleen and about dating in general. In his own words, "I yearned to come to this country for studies and such. I knew there were cultural differences. I grew up in a culture where dating was taboo, and you never went on a date. The whole concept of dating was new to me. I am used to being the golden boy in the family and living by the rules." There was a sense of adventure and an element of "just having a bit of fun" early on in their relationship. Once their relationship turned serious with the hopes of it becoming a long-term partnership, Shiva was faced with a major decision.

Shiva's family is an orthodox Tamil Iyer Hindu family. The *Iyer* religious community is one of two conservative orthodox Brahmin religious sects in South India; the other is *Iyengar*, which is the tradition of my husband's family. Likely in the next year or two, as Shiva came close to achieving his PhD in the United States, his parents would have created a profile for their son to circulate among the subcaste Iyer Tamil community of eligible women around India and the USA. They knew their son would have been a most sought-after match because he was educated in America with a PhD in engineering and would likely be working in the United States in a lucrative field. Shiva knew his relationship with this *western woman* would not be received well, and it would mean a dramatic shift in how his parents viewed him as their eldest son. Consequently, they broke up. Colleen was disheartened, especially when she learned that Shiva's parents would be arranging his marriage. She recalls, "I thought that there might be a possibility with Shiva and a relationship evolving when he stated so definitively, 'My family will be arranging a marriage.' That was like, you know, the road just stopped." Particularly true for Tamilian Hindu young adults who travel abroad for advanced education, when they meet someone outside their cultural context and date for the first time, these "love" relationships may end in heartbreak because the family ties and expectations to *marry within the community* are so strong; the risk to the individual to defy these norms become too great to bear long-term.

His family's objections were based on a number of factors: her age, her religion, her marital status, as well as her culture. "They felt the gaps were just too big. In our case they felt like it would be a disaster because she's already been married before, and she comes from a family that has gone through divorces. There's an age difference. There's cultural differences," Shiva explains his parent's rationale for opposing their relationship. They went to great lengths to prevent their relationship from moving forward. Colleen and Shiva traveled to India to introduce her to the family. His parents refused to travel within India with Colleen, for fear that others would see them together and ask questions. And on the occasion when she was in the car with them, they explained to the taxi driver that she was Shiva's professor—which, of course, she was not. They wrote letters to Shiva's doctoral advisor asking him "to intervene and talk sense" into Shiva. They wrote letters to Colleen's dad asking him to stop the relationship as well. Colleen recalls, "My dad said he would never share the letters with me, that they were hateful towards me. My dad was incredibly upset, and I don't think he ever forgave them for that." The four of them on Colleen's first trip to India traveled separately to an ashram where his parents felt comfortable. While at the Sai Baba ashram, Shiva recalls a conversation with one of the respected leaders of the movement and who was also friends of the family. This spiritual advisor was educated in the West himself; therefore Shiva was surprised by what he said to him on this trip. "They took me to one of their advisors who was talking to me about 'beware of the traps of the Western Woman.'" *Beware of the traps of the Western Woman* is the message that came across loud and clear. One can hear a tale meant to engender *fear of the foreigner*. Western women ensnare Indian boys and lead them astray, away from their families and from their responsibilities. My own in-laws questioned my husband before we were married, asking if he was marrying me for my money, as if I was enticing him in some way. The irony is that I was poor and came from a poor family. For Shiva's parents, this was more than a conflict between religions, or a difference of caste, or race; this was a conflict between competing cultures and the values they promote.

Colleen's family was not eager to support their relationship either. They were concerned about the patriarchal views of the family she was marrying into. They also had misconceptions about Hinduism and conflated it with religious stereotypes they had heard about conservative Muslim communities. "My sister clumped Indians and Pakistanis into one category and said, 'They're very chauvinistic and you don't want to be with a chauvinist.'" Colleen continues, "My dad was very concerned. He's like, 'I raised you to be an independent woman and it seems to me that there's a lot of chauvinism. It's too patriarchal, that's not who you are.'"

WHEN NATIONAL IDENTITY AND BORDER POLITICS MATTER

As I stood in front of my congregation at our annual meeting on February 5, 2017, my heart was racing as we prepared to take a ballot vote on becoming an "Immigrant Welcoming" congregation. We spent the previous year, engaged as a congregation, in deeper study exploring immigration patterns within Wisconsin and learning what the Bible has to say about welcoming the stranger. We learned about border politics in the United States and identified our own immigration narratives from our family histories. On this day we were faced with a clear choice to declare on whose side we would stand as a congregation—the side of the immigrant and refugee or the side of national safety and security for our country. The intensity in my United Church of Christ congregation was high regarding our vote, because, nine days earlier, then President Trump signed and released Executive Order 13769, "Protecting the Nation from Foreign Terrorist Entry into the United States,"[8] known commonly as the Muslim Ban. Barred from entry were people coming to the United States from Iran, Iraq, Libya, Somalia, Sudan, Syria, and Yemen, which are predominately Muslim countries. The day before, February 4, I was one of the leaders to speak at a #NoBanNoWall

---

8. Trump, "Protecting the Nation."

protest rally in Janesville, with nearly one thousand people present.[9] After the rally, we marched a few blocks to Representative Paul Ryan's office, who was then the Speaker of the House of Representatives. We were there to urge him to oppose the president's discriminatory policy against Muslims traveling to the United States. Among those prevented from entering the US was the wife and new baby of my husband's direct report, who was prevented from returning from Iran to her husband and to their home in Chicago. The Muslim ban was affecting not only visitors and refugees, but also the lives of people across the country who lived and worked in the United States.

Not everyone at that congregational annual meeting in Janesville was for this new immigrant welcoming policy. I knew there would be opposition, but I had not thought what it would mean to me if the vote did not pass. It was an ontological moment for me, a defining moment in my own religious identity. *This was not only political, or even just a matter of religion. This was personal.* A vote to welcome immigrants and to work for policies and programs that advocate for immigrants, regardless of their status, was personal because my husband was an immigrant. Are immigrants welcome here? The personal was political, the political was personal, and it was a matter of faith and politics in my own life and ministry. This is a central question that people of faith are wrestling with across our country—*who is welcome here? Who is welcome into our country? Who is welcome to live in our communities? Who is welcome to belong within our congregations?* These are questions of identity—national identity, religious identity, and cultural identity.

Flashpoint: The Muslim Ban Incident

Between January 28, and February 5, 2017, #NoBanNoWall rallies were a national public response opposing the Muslim Ban (a.k.a Executive Order 13769), which banned entry from seven primarily Muslim countries. This became a flashpoint for activism against xenophobia and religious hate speech and violence. It sparked national and international conversations about religion and national origin as potential barriers for exclusion based in an argument for protectionism, safety, and security against Islamic terrorists. During Trump's presidential campaign, our congregation helped to establish the "Love Over Fear" counter-campaign articulating a message

9. Johnson, "Hundreds Protest Trump."

that faith communities must not succumb to the fear-inciting rhetoric that was being harbored by the political candidates, none louder than candidate Trump himself. In December 2015, during the presidential campaign cycle, we joined with churches, synagogues, and mosques, as well as other communities of faith in Madison, Wisconsin, creating the hashtag "#LoveOverFear," which was then shared in social media posts and on yard signs placed on church properties and in residential neighborhoods. We were opposed to the hate speech being heard in the campaigns against refugees fleeing war. The subsequent federal ban on all foreigners from these overwhelmingly Muslim countries sent a clear message to those who supported President Trump during the campaign—he will keep America safe from *those outsiders* and so-called terrorists. The tactic to stoke fires of fear of the stranger and declaring that the Muslim outsider is dangerous, however, emboldened people of faith, including progressive Christians, Muslim, and Jewish communities, to take a stand against this xenophobic rhetoric.

After 9/11 violence against Muslims, Sikhs, and others of South Asian and Middle Eastern origin increased and then increased again with the 2016 election. This would be the beginning of a new wave of violence we would see over the coming four years against Muslims, Sikhs, and Arabs, as well as anti-Semitic violence against Jews. According to "Communities on Fire," published by the SAALT (South Asian Americans Leading Together), violence and hate crimes against South Asian Americans increased by 64 percent in the first year after President Trump was elected.

> The current climate of Islamophobia is both a product of the steady growth in white supremacist organizations and movements as well as the Trump administration's rhetoric and policies, which have provided a vehicle to operationalize white supremacist priorities on a national scale. There is undoubtedly a strong connection between hate incidents and President Trump's xenophobic political rhetoric. Of the 213 documented incidents of hate violence postelection, perpetrators in approximately 1 out of every 5 incidents (21%) referenced President Trump, a Trump policy, or a Trump campaign slogan.[10]

Janesville was only one community among many across the nation that was protesting President Trump's hastily written immigration ban that was released on January 27, 2017. These protests began at Kennedy International Airport, after the detaining of two Iraqi refugees, according to the *New York*

10. Modi et al., "Communities on Fire."

The History of Us versus Them

Times, and then swelled to dozens of other airports and cities over the next ten days.[11] Given that Rep. Paul Ryan was the Speaker of the House at the time, Janesville became a focal point for people's outrage against the travel ban and our role as a nation to be welcoming to immigrants and refugees.

These border politics and accompanying protests highlighted strong opinions across the political and religious spectrums. February of 2017 brought the #NoBanNoWall protests to my own backyard.[12] These were not just political rhetorical movements or discriminatory policies on religious groups. This amounted to an invitation to xenophobic white citizens to lash out at anyone who seemed to fit the description of *the Muslim other*. The hateful rhetoric has everyday consequences for people who live at the intersection of racial, religious, and national identities. The challenges these couples faced were impacted by even larger governmental forces at work, including the US governmental policies in El Salvador, India's partition and subsequent wars drawing the borders of East and West Pakistan, as well as a shift from more permeable borders to tighter US immigration laws and sentiments today. National identity and border politics matter in the everyday lives of multicultural interfaith couples. These are the questions at the heart of identity—who belongs here, who is welcome here, and who can stay here.

Multicultural interfaith couples often make uncommon friends. Paul and Cathy have relationships that are both ecumenical, spanning multiple Christian traditions, and interreligious, including people from Buddhist and Jewish traditions. It was early on in their relationship when they went to a gathering at their local Quaker meeting house and were introduced to students who were Salvadoran refugees fleeing violence. This was a transformative experience for the couple and propelled them to action. In February of 1983, Cathy remembers, "We left that night after listening to these two university students give their testimony of how their university was attacked by the military. Many of them had been threatened, so they were fleeing for safety. We left that night saying, wow, kind of feeling called. We knew we needed to do something." They felt *called to action*, and thus began their work with the Sanctuary movement. Ultimately, they became witnesses for the abuse and violence that was taking place in El Salvador through their participation with CRISPAZ—Christians for Peace in El Salvador.

11. Rosenberg, "Protest Grows."
12. Newman, "Highlights: Reaction."

This was no longer about fighting the religious institution; this was about resisting and exposing the US governmental policies and practices against the poor and marginalized in El Salvador. Paul describes this eye-opening experience, "So many others were being persecuted and they were *illegal* in our country. We saw that our government was responsible. That's what really hit, I think for both of us, that *we Americans were responsible*. Our government was sending down military aid to the tune of a million [dollars a day]." Despite a "bloody civil war" going on, Paul and Cathy were connected with the right people, and thus began what would become annual trips to El Salvador for the next thirty-five years. He continues, "What we did, mainly, was gather information on what was actually happening in El Salvador, taking pictures. We couldn't take pictures at that time in the open. And so, we did it on the sly. Then we came back, and we started to give talks to whomever would listen to us about how our money is being used in El Salvador to oppress people and to support things like death squads." They helped form coalitions of thirty churches and faith communities to become part of the Sanctuary movement to shelter these *illegal aliens* fleeing El Salvador, who were seeking refuge in the United States. Paul and Cathy were witnesses. They raised awareness and educated others about the conditions of people from within these religious orders, often within seminaries and institutions of higher education, who were being abducted for their efforts to "organize nonviolently to get better, clean water, electricity, you know, basic, basic human needs." They advocated with their state representatives through calls and letter-writing campaigns for implementation of the immigration laws that were not being followed at the time, with regards to Salvadoran refugees. Their faith compelled them to take action.

12

Leaders for Change, Movements for Justice

EARLY IN MY SEMINARY education, in 2003, I joined another local seminarian, who belonged to the Methodist church, in planning an "Interfaith Youth Day of Service" in northwest Indiana. He had connections with local Christian congregations and youth groups, and I was able to connect to our Hindu high school youth through my family's participation in our local Chinmaya Mission chapter. The first year was a success and, as the second year planning got underway, I was invited to take on the leadership role. The youth from these various religious traditions went home and told their parents about their day of learning about one another's religious traditions and working together on a variety of community service projects. The parents wanted to participate. In 2004, in partnership with my local PCUSA congregation and our Habitat for Humanity chapter, I soon founded the Northwest Indiana Interfaith Habitat for Humanity Building Project, the first of its kind in the country. Over three weekends, Buddhists, Christians, Jews, Hindus, and Muslims came together to build a house for a young African American single mother in Gary, Indiana. With daily meditations, space for prayer, and a shared lunch together, we worked side by side across race, gender, and religion and worked towards the common goal of supporting a young family having a beautiful new home. Later that year I attended the National Youth Core's conference and presented our work. There I met Eboo Patel.

From Outlaw to In-law

Interfaith Leadership: A Primer by Patel shows the power of dialogue coupled with acts of service to impact religious communities and people in positive ways. In this book, Patel argues for the value of a particular kind of leadership that utilizes the tenets from dialogue and cooperation he shepherded within the Interfaith Youth Core over the years. He highlights the "Vision of Interfaith Leadership" to include (1) respect for identity; (2) relationships between different communities; and (3) a commitment to the common good.[1] Patel spends some time speaking to the benefits of working for the common good and defines it as "principles and structures that a range of groups benefit from and people generally agree we have a collective interest to uphold."[2] As it applies to interfaith leadership, the common good is five-fold:

1. Increasing understanding and reducing prejudice.
2. Strengthening social cohesion and reducing the chances for identity-based conflict.
3. Bridging social capital and addressing social problems.
4. Fostering the continuity of identity communities and reducing isolation.
5. Creating biding narratives for diverse societies.[3]

Patel is arguing for a methodology of reducing prejudice and conflict through activities that invite participants across faith traditions into community service. He is calling forth leaders to be the social change agents for this kind of *interfaith leadership* that promotes deeper connections and understanding across diverse religious traditions. The Interfaith Youth Core was most effective on college campuses where there was a greater density of religious diversity and, therefore, opportunities for collaborative projects. In communities where there is little religious diversity, these kinds of projects would naturally bear less fruit.

In northwest Indiana, where I lived at the time, being a suburb of Chicago, we were able to draw on high school students to participate because of the diversity within our own community. To say that our project met the idealistic notions of common good and cooperation Patel outlines would be to sugarcoat the real challenges we faced. Our work, for instance, was not sustainable because of a movement within the older, more established

---

1. Patel, *Interfaith Leadership*, 93–96.
2. Patel, *Interfaith Leadership*, 96.
3. Patel, *Interfaith Leadership*, 98–99.

faith traditions—Christian and Jewish—to limit participation in interfaith activities to communities whose places of worship were located within a particular town. It so happened that the brown and Black communities who joined in the Interfaith Habitat for Humanity Build were our Hindu and Muslim participants. Their places of worship were not in that mostly white town. Their places of worship were located nearby, where land was less expensive and available at the time of those communities' formation. The more powerful *white faith traditions* created a policy that was implicitly racist. Inspired by Paul Knitter, who reviewed his book, Patel calls for a *theology of interfaith cooperation* that utilizes a variety of faith traditions, such as Gandhi's nonviolence movement; the Jewish concept of *tzaddik*, who is "a righteous one"; and the Islamic idea of *ayat,* in which Patel says, "God gives us his signs in many places," including signs from other religious traditions.[4] Patel falls short of curating an interfaith theology of cooperation, but he is an organizer and leader of action and not a theologian.

We can take important lessons from Patel as we consider the value our multicultural interfaith couples may bring to our conversation of social change agency and interfaith religious engagement. The skills developed by working through conflict, prejudice, and discrimination can become valuable tools for future leadership. Patel begins to identify what those shared values might be between people of different religious traditions, but does not take into consideration the unique relationship that happens within interfaith families who engage in dialogue and acts of service shared over a lifetime together.

We are living in what I call the "New Prophetic Age." This New Prophetic Age is marked by the rise of social movements with people of faith at the heart of them. Leaders within these movements are often people whose lives are considered to be at the margins of society—or at least they are usually not white cisgendered men of privilege and power. The environmental movement received new energy from a new generation when Greta Thunberg began her School Strikes for Climate Change. Black American woman Tarana Burke began the MeToo movement in 2006, when she began using the phrase to encourage women to speak out against their sexual abuse. Actress Alyssa Milano picked up "me too" as a hashtag (#MeToo) on Twitter a decade later, in 2017, during the sexual abuse allegations against Harvey Weinstein. The March for Our Lives gun control movement was started by high school students who witnessed the shooting at Marjory Stoneman

4. Patel, *Interfaith Leadership*, 11–122.

Douglas High School on February 14, 2018. It is notable that students who could not vote were the ones who began marching and protesting for sensible gun laws. We are facing some of the most challenging complex issues of our time: gun violence and school shootings, calls for racial equity, immigration disputes and a global refugee crisis, ongoing religious strife between traditions, queer rights and a call for gender inclusivity, and demands for climate justice to save our planet from destruction. These are the movements with leaders who rise from the margins that are making some of the largest positive impacts in our social world today.

The Black Lives Matter protests, the #MeToo campaign, LGBTQ+ rights, #NoBanNoWall rallies, and #MarchforOurLives walk-outs are a few of the social movements where people of goodwill put their faith into action. They are making a difference. These kinds of actions demonstrate that we can still affect positive change in our communities. This is social change for the common good. These people are the prophets of our time, often rising from the margins of our communities with leaders who are able point to the disenfranchisement of many and speak their truth to those in power in order to affect positive changes. Some seek inclusion, some seek dignity and equal rights, others seek a place at the decision-making table. These movements comprise people from diverse communities across race, religion, nationality, and culture.

There are often deep divides between cultural norms, religious perspectives, or even barriers of language and ethnic origins. We need more leaders who can bridge these differences, think innovatively, and act prophetically. I do not mean that we need more leaders of new movements. What I mean is that if we are to affect change in our society at the level of families and communities, we need more everyday people showing leadership during these complex social and cultural times we live in. These leaders may rise from multicultural interfaith couples and families. These multicultural interfaith couples may bring the kind of nuanced leadership our world needs today. There seems to be a global movement for equity and inclusion upon us and it is designed to seek the flourishing of our siblings who find themselves disinherited and disenfranchised. Successful social movements need innovative leadership to do this work of faith-based justice. Our local communities need nuanced leaders too, in our schools, in our city governments, in our companies, and within our religious communities. Couples who have been put on the margins of their communities because of not belonging fully to one religion or another, one racial group or another, one culture or another, should be at the center of our conversations. When we talk about diversity, equity, and inclusion, people who have lived lives facing daily discrimination and prejudice because of the intersectionality of their marriages may have specialized insight into how we might bridge the gaps that separate us from one another.

A SURVEY OF MULTICULTURAL INTERFAITH COUPLES

As part of my research, I reached out to multicultural interfaith couples around the world using a survey. My efforts resulted in fifty-six couples responding. Multicultural interfaith couples may become agents of social change, because of the skills they learn from living inside of multiracial, interreligious, and cross-cultural families and from dealing with the prejudice and discrimination they experience within their communities. I wanted to learn more about their experiences.

Some people found my survey through a variety of means: word of mouth, by reading my blog, seeing my posts or comments on Reddit, or by posts through friendship networks or the Interfaith Family Network groups on Facebook. The demographics of those who responded to the survey represent a very diverse group of couples. In total, fifty-six couples took the survey, representing 112 people of diverse religious, cultural, national, class, and racial backgrounds. They reside in eleven different countries: Canada, China, Costa Rica, France, India, Japan, the Netherlands, Poland, Thailand, the United Kingdom, and the United States of America, within which, respondents reside in nineteen different states. The years the couples were married ranged from recently engaged to married more than twenty years, with twenty-six respondents reporting being married zero to five years; six married five to ten years; seven married ten to fifteen years; nine married fifteen to twenty years; and six who have been married more than twenty years. It is interesting to note that 76 percent of the couples had children who were under twenty years of age.

Table 12.1 Religious Affiliation of Couples Surveyed

Religious Affiliation of at least One Member of the Couple	Percentage of Couples	# of Couples
Christian/Catholic	69%	38
Muslim	45%	25
Hindu	25%	14
Jewish	14%	8
Buddhist	9%	5
Sikh	9%	5
Unitarian Universalists	5%	3
No Religious Affiliation	5%	3
Multiple Religious Affiliations	21%	12
Agnostic or Atheist	14%	8

The most remarkable demographic among those who responded lies with the diversity of their religious affiliations. Not surprisingly, the largest group of interfaith couples that completed the survey had at least one member of their couple that was Christian (Catholic or Protestant), representing 69 percent of survey respondents. Muslim interfaith couples were the second largest group of interfaith couples that responded; 45 percent of those couples surveyed had at least one member who identified as Muslim. Hindu interfaith couples came in third at 25 percent of those surveyed with at least one member who identified as Hindu. Jewish interfaith couples came in at 14 percent. Buddhist interfaith couples and Sikh interfaith couples both came in at 9 percent of the total surveyed. Those who listed Unitarian Universalists among their religious affiliations numbered 5 percent, along with those who claimed no religious affiliation at all. Importantly, 21 percent of the couples reported at least one person identified with more than one religious affiliation. Using Bidwell's terminology to describe these couples, 21 percent of those surveyed would fall within the category of the spiritually fluid. Finally, it is worthy to note that 14 percent of the interfaith couples surveyed had at least one member who identified as agnostic or atheist. Note the percentages listed above add up to more than 100 percent, because there is overlap between the religious affiliations.

There was racial and ethnic diversity within the population of those who responded to the survey. Of the 112 people from the fifty-six couples surveyed, they were asked to identify their ethnicity and respond to a question about the "tone or color of their skin" as a way to measure how someone appears in public. Of 108 people who responded to the question of ethnicity, the percentages of those identities are found Table 12.2 Race/Ethnicity of Couples Surveyed.

Table 12.2 Race/Ethnicity of Couples Surveyed

Percent	Race/Ethnicity	# of respondents Out of 108
48%	White	52
25%	Asian Indian/Indian Origin	27
5%	Black	6
5%	Southeast Asian	5
2%	Hispanic/Lantinx	2
2%	Far East Asian	2
13%	Multiple Ethnic Identities	14
100%		=108

The predominant ethnic groups represented in descending order include white, Asian Indian, Black and Southeast Asian, with Latinx people representing only 2 percent of respondents. However, 13 percent of respondents report belonging to more than one ethnic group. Included among these responses were people who identified as a combination of ethnicities, which included Arab, Middle Eastern, North African, and Filipino.

A STATEMENT ON LEADERSHIP

As we look for nuanced leadership in our world today to bridge conflicts around race, culture, religion, class and national divides, perhaps an untapped source of social change agency and leadership may come from multicultural interfaith couples who have had to navigate the harsh reality of border politics, racial tensions, culture wars, and religious conflicts. These negative experiences come from their own family members, religious leaders, and coworkers. These experiences are often directed at them precisely because of their choice of marriage partner. Once beloved members of their own communities, people who love across the boundaries of race, culture, class, caste, and religion, may cause generational conflicts. The life they choose may undermine and destroy what their parents and community value most. Many experience an identity crisis as they face the reality that who they love is not welcome and does not belong within their community.

The act of standing up for the dignity and worth of their *othered* partner time and time again in multiple circumstances and contexts may itself become a source of social change not only within the couple but, more importantly, within their surrounding communities. Our couples' sense of self, religious and cultural identity, as well as racial and national sensitivity all expand to adapt to and include their partner's differences. Marrying across culture, race, religion, and national identity may deepen one's faith, and the ability to respond compassionately to complex social situations.

The New Prophetic Age is a time of movements for justice and inclusion, and people whose calls for dignity and equal treatment are now being heard. For example, calls for racial justice, marriage equality, distribution of wealth, and gender equity are shaping new policies at both the local and national levels of the United States. Political campaigns are being held accountable by those whose voices would not normally be center stage. The #MeToo movement has the power to unmask sexual harassment cases and unseat men who have been shielded too long. This is the kind of work that the new prophets are doing in our time. In other words, people from the margins are speaking truth to those who hold power—and those same marginalized voices, in some cases, are now assuming new roles of power.

The role of the prophet is not just reserved for political and religious leadership. Anyone can rise up and lead us into a new future that is *more just, more inclusive,* and *more loving.* Who is a prophet? What is the prophet's role? How can these ideas about prophetic leadership support those who are committed to empowering their communities to work for positive social change? Walter Brueggemann, in *The Prophetic Imagination,* says this, "The task of prophetic imagination and ministry is *to bring public expression those very hopes and yearnings* that have been denied so long and suppressed so deeply that we no longer know they are there."[5] He suggests that this compassion is actually "a radical form of criticism"[6] against the dominant cultural consciousness, and this is precisely the power within the revelatory acts of Jesus' ministry. By showing compassion and engaging in public lament and hopeful visioning, Jesus made real the pain of the oppressed community showing forth the "*ache* of God" that can "penetrate the *numbness* of history."[7] This is transforming love that leads the least, the lost, and the lonely toward liberating love.

---

5. Brueggemann, *Prophetic Imagination,* 65. Emphasis original.
6. Brueggemann, *Prophetic Imagination,* 88.
7. Brueggemann, *Prophetic Imagination,* 55.

Prophetic leadership invites us to use all aspects of our usual and customary work to inspire people to connect their lives toward the work of liberating love.[8] Expanding our ideas of what counts as prophetic work beyond traditional ministry to people within multicultural interfaith couples, then acting in solidarity and witness, accompanying in the form of political protest and rallies, as well as being in mentorship relationships and creating experiences of cross-cultural encounters all become opportunities to demonstrate leadership and prophetic activism. This kind of work encourages one to use their own faith for the benefit of those whose voices have been left out and pushed out. *An important value of prophetic leadership is to promote inclusion and the dignity of all.* With respect to this research, one finds their way to advocating for the dignity and worth of those who are *othered* outside of their family by first beginning to fight for the dignity and worth of their partner. Advocating for other *othered people* in the larger community grows outward from those experiences with one's partner at home.

---

8. Brueggemann, *Prophetic Imagination*, 4.

13

Seeking Justice for Others

Social change agency is the freedom to stand up against injustice in all its forms, in part because we have learned to stand up for our partners, who were once outsiders and outcasts. At the heart of this work is an exploration of how long-term interfaith dialogue between partners within a committed relationship creates the conditions for them to become positive social change agents in their families and communities. Social change agency is the ability to take actions that lead families, communities, and organizations toward adapting to changing environmental and social factors, such as the changing landscape of racially mixed communities and multifaith families. Social change agency is a person's ability to, through personal stories or cultural requests, encourage these families, communities, and organizations to consider adopting new policies, practices, or even products that welcome the outsider into the community. Social change agency, in this context, refers to the presence of the couple who challenges norms in a way that invites positive change moving toward inclusion and welcoming of those who were once thought of as strange.

Social change agency is one way of considering a person's ability to change the perspectives and actions of others around them, who may hold misconceptions, prejudices, or have discriminatory policies in place regarding race, culture, nationality, or religion. My survey attempts to measure the ways in which multicultural interfaith couples are easily and regularly engaged in social change activities. Another way to ask this question is simply this: *Are multicultural interfaith couples potential leaders for social change in their communities?*

MEASURING SOCIAL CHANGE AGENCY

Social change agency can be thought of as a qualitative concept. I saught to measure social change agency through a series of questions that focus on six distinct factors: (1) the impact a couple has had on changing their family's views toward their multicultural interfaith relationship; (2) seeking exceptions to a rule or policy for their family or others that they perceived were unfair based on culture/race/caste/class/religion; (3) participation in voluntary organizations and activities; (4) participating in social justice activities or social movements, or leadership of such activities; (5) advocating for the rights of others who they perceived were being treated unfairly based on race, class, caste, or religious affiliation; and, finally, (6) the extent to which they have grown in their own faith over the life of their relationship.

Regarding their ability to change the perspective of their families' views of their own multicultural interfaith relationship the survey asked: "Would you say that your family's views (or your partner's family's views) of your relationship have changed over time?" This question highlighted the positive or negative views their respective families may have had about their relationship, but, more importantly, it points to possible growth. More than 50 percent of these couples reported that their families' view of their relationship had changed and their families had grown to accept and appreciate their relationship over time. The questions about seeking an exception to a rule or policy for themselves or others did not bear fruit, with most answering no. I believe this question could be improved upon in future studies of this kind. Perhaps a better approach would have been to ask a series of questions about specific kinds of rules or policies that tend to discriminate against people of color, a person's culture, or their religious belonging. Participation in volunteer activities was a short-answer fill-in-the-blank question with five open slots for answers. Not all answered this question; some only put one or two activities. However, 47 percent listed three or more kinds of voluntary activities that they were engaged in, suggesting that these couples were involved in multiple kinds of social change activities through their volunteerism.

Participation in recent social movements and social justice activities proved to be an interesting question. Not only did 54 percent say that they participated in social movements or social justice activities, twenty-seven couples, or 48 percent of those surveyed, listed specific movements in which they had participated. Among those activities listed, many highlighted participation in racial equity activities and Black Lives Matters marches,

marches against the Muslim Ban or working across faiths for immigration reform, March for Our Lives against Gun Violence, the 2017 Women's March, Take Back the Night rallies and other programs for gender equity, participation in political campaigns, Gay Pride marches and LGBTQ advocacy groups, participation in the Sanctuary movement and lobbying work, and activities advocating for climate justice. In addition to participating in movements or social justice activities, the survey asked about advocating for the rights of another who they perceived were being treated unfairly by the system based on their race, caste, class, or religious affiliation. Fifty-seven percent of those surveyed said that they had advocated for the rights of another and, of those, 52 percent attributed their interfaith relationship as helping them to understand better the specific situation. These couples can see that their personal relationship with their partner of a different culture and religion supported their ability to understand another person's unfair situation, and, then, allowed them to better advocate on that person's behalf. This is a significant result gained from the survey, and worthy of further investigation.

The final measure of social change agency is the impact that their relationship has had on their own faith and spirituality. Knitter, Miller, Patel, and others have suggested that interfaith dialogue does not dilute or take away from one's faith or religious engagement. Rather, interfaith dialogue tends to deepen one's own experience of their faith and the connection to their religious tradition. My survey results would seem to support those assertions. Among the multicultural interfaith couples who participated in my survey, 52 percent reported that at least one member of their couple grew in their faith over the course of their relationship. When you consider which couples experienced both partners growing in their faith, 41 percent reported growth in their faith over the life of their partnership among both members of the couple. Multicultural interfaith marriages can have significant impact in their communities and, I believe, are agents of a variety of positive changes within their families, communities, and the institutions around them.

Social change agency allows multicultural interfaith couples to understand complex and, often, difficult situations, and to stand in the face of conflict between people and not shy away. In their perseverance with Shiva's orthodox parents, Colleen and Shiva learned to stand up against oppression and to seek solutions that others may not have thought possible. For example, Colleen stepped in and advocated for a grocery store worker who was being verbally abused by a customer. In a work conference she silenced homophobic remarks being made at her table among colleagues about a gay coworker, who was not present. Similarly, Shiva will speak up on matters that he would not normally have done in the past. He explains, before he married Colleen, "I was so afraid of conflict, desperately. But if presented with the conflict now, I don't think we shy away from it."

Paul and Cathy, the spiritually fluid Buddhist-Catholic/Buddhist couple, saw incredible suffering in El Salvador and, yet, from these same persecuted Salvadoran citizens, they saw amazing spiritual resilience. The people were daily struggling to survive against the well-funded military who were targeting these seminarians for just trying to *do something good* in their communities. While in El Salvador, Paul and Cathy were not immune to the violence. They told me the story of their most frightening encounters:

> Paul: We didn't go where we were not supposed to go. We were always with other Salvadorans who knew the terrain up to a point. There were times when it got a little bit dicey, when there was a firefight broke out between the FMLN [the Farabundo Martí National Liberation Front][1] and the rebels and the locals. We were, we were at a retreat house and it was going on around us. We were under the bed, you know.
>
> Cathy: That was the worst.
>
> Paul: That was the worst.
>
> Cathy: Well, or the time we get taken off the bus, but anyhow . . .
>
> Paul: Yea, that was another time we got taken off the bus by the military. But it was, it was a vital part of our relationship, namely, that we were committed to something, you know, that *we felt just called*.

They were *called to do something*. When asked how they could face this level of violence and threats, they explained how their respective faith traditions contributed to their activism. For Paul, it was his own practice of *liberation theology*. "That was how I understood my Christian faith, that salvation includes human fulfillment. '*Gloria Dei est vivens homo*'; 'the glory of God is humanity fully alive,' as Saint Irenaeus put it. Out in these villages of abject poverty and you see these people coming around to read the Bible to find strength and guidance. It was just a profound inspiration for my faith then." For Cathy, she shares that she was moved by what she witnessed. For

---

1. The FMNL is a Salvadoran political party and former guerrilla rebel group.

her, "witnessing that level of commitment and the ability to contextualize their spiritual experience amidst so much suffering and injustice, that really moved me." Her Buddhist practice helped in her peace activism as well as in her ability to witness suffering. She explains, "I find that the practices, the compassion practices, extremely helpful in sitting with and witnessing suffering. Not jumping in to try to act or fix or help. There are various practices; *tonglen* is one of them. Sitting with and being really in empathy with another's suffering." Both inspired by the Salvadoran people and empowered by their respective faith traditions, this couple's deep religious engagement within and across their religious traditions compelled them to become advocates for social change across the border within El Salvador as well as within the United States. Their focus included trying to reform the US implementation of the immigration laws. Compassionate leaders and faithful witnesses, together for over forty years, Paul and Cathy are not alone in their profound caring and agency for social change. This level of commitment can be found within couples who are just starting out together.

Kamran is a software engineer and Kamalpreet works in human resources. Not yet married, this couple is not shy to speak of their social change agency. They both use their professional skills to work toward equity and justice for others who have fewer opportunities. Kamran mentors at-risk youth in his community, in a program called "Year Up." In this year-long program, these youth learn professional skills and secure employment. The mentors teach the youth technical skills, then the program pairs them with a six-month, forty-hour-a-week job where they can develop and hone those newly formed skills. Kamalpreet is proud to sponsor a girl through World Vision and watch as she grows and develops. A self-described "huge feminist," she has created women-in-technology groups to bring women back into the workforce. "I am a strong believer of equality. I want to do things that help cultures and communities that are unrepresented or underrepresented, or do not have enough, or just don't have the opportunities." When police violence became a national conversation during the Black Lives Matter protests the summer of 2020, Kamran mobilized a group of his peers to design a software application for phones to keep the public informed about places where police brutality was more of a problem. He explains, "I actually do work to support those movements, not just like passive support. Back in July, I gathered a bunch of software engineers to help me on building this app that tells you about police killings all over the country. It tells you what state, what city, which police departments are having the highest, most problematic [incidents]. I did it for a political activist group." He is keen to point out the on-again, off-again tendency of people who join a movement for a short period, posting on social media and attending a march, but who show little long-term commitment to making an impact in a social justice issue. Kamran values simplicity and "is a big proponent of minimalism and gratitude" and wants to do something about the problems he sees in the world. Kamalpreet wants to empower women and girls to help them be successful. They are beginning their lives together as active agents of social change within their networks. One wonders what kind of lasting impact and leadership they will bring as their married years unfold over time.

14

Reimagining Faith and God

INTERFAITH DIALOGUE IMAGINES TWO people of different faith traditions engaging in a conversation about their faith, beliefs, concept of God, what is sacred, and religious practices. We can imagine a certain curiosity and cordiality between these two people, maybe at an academic symposium or over coffee. They sit for a time sharing their differences, discovering their similarities, and then go home to their families and enclaves of familiarity and uniformity. In an interfaith couple there is no "going home" after the dialogue is done. The conflicts and differences that arise are matters of utmost importance. How they navigate the belief differences has impact on their weekly routines, their life-cycle rituals, and their ability to raise their children within one or both religious traditions. Talking about faith and God are both enriching and dangerous endeavors. It requires trust, forgiveness, compassion, and respect. When who you love can be thought of as the enemy in your larger family, it is of paramount importance that you understand who they are, what they believe, and can advocate for their right to belong in a situation where they would be considered an outsider.

Talking about God and our faith broadens our understanding of not just our partner's faith and traditions. It deepens our understanding of our faith and traditions because it affords us the opportunity to reevaluate those beliefs in light of our values and commitments inside of a multicultural interfaith relationship. We are changed by the dialogue. New beliefs may emerge. Who we know ourselves to be *ontologically* shifts in the process of engaging in long-term committed conversations with our partner and their extended family. Reimagining our faith and what we believe about God is one of the blessings of living inside of a multicultural interfaith family.

Our newly married Taiwanese Christian/American Hindu couple began to explore each other's religious traditions in the beginning of their relationship. They had lots of questions for one another. "It started with Peter buying me Christian apologists' books," Geetha commented. Peter spoke about his evolving faith this way.

> I feel like growing up in the Evangelical Christian household, you have a very particular way of thinking about Christianity as a religion. I went to an Evangelical Christian college. I started seeing Geetha and engaged in this kind dialogue. This has expanded my perspective on Christianity. The process started with Geetha asking a lot of questions about Christian faith like, 'Does God, like the one described in the Bible, truly exist? Who wrote the Bible? Has Jesus resurrected? How accurate is history as told in the Bible? What is sin?' and these often turned into debates in the beginning.
>
> Through that dialogue in that old Evangelical version of myself, my intention, at the time, was "hopefully she can convert." Then, that would be easier for me to present that relationship to my parents. Through the process of conversing about those questions about faith, I started to learn those are legit questions. I don't necessarily have the answer to those. I started thinking more. I found the other side of the spectrum and more liberal theology and, eventually, that helped me to be more receptive and accepting of other faiths and also be more open to learn about other religions.

Peter's Christian faith expanded to become more inclusive of other traditions. His commitment to convert his Hindu wife to Christianity fell away. He learned in the process how their two cultures and faith traditions could coexist in their household and be valued and appreciated. Peter describes these conversations as "really great." Geetha said it this way, "I found the whole process quite enriching. It was a good exercise in biblical scholarship."

For this couple, planning the wedding ceremonies to include both cultures and families' religious traditions took extra work and allowed them to grow further in their understanding of their traditions, as well as allowed them to adapt the ceremonies to fit their values, which were distinct from their parents. Geetha reflects on that process.

> Trying to customize the Hindu ceremony, trying to understand all the chanting and the religious rituals that happen was a challenge.

> I have to work a little bit harder so that I can explain it to you. I don't know if I was successful. Just trying to find the translations of all the chanting you do in a wedding ceremony was hard. I don't think I would have gone through that effort if I was marrying another TamBram.

Geetha uses the term "TamBram" here, which refers to other Tamil Brahmin Hindus. Meaning, it would not be necessary to translate the Sanskrit *slokas* customarily chanted at the wedding when you marry inside of the particular faith and caste community of her parents. Ironically, what is being chanted is not understood by the couple even when they speak Tamil because the priest chants them in an ancient scriptural language, Sanskrit. They would not question the priest or take the time to learn the meaning of what would be said at their wedding ceremony by the priest. Because Geetha was marrying outside of that community, it took more work, but those efforts allowed her to grow in her own understanding of her faith tradition while being able to explain what was happening to Peter and then to his parents. I attended their wedding, given Geetha is my husband's niece. They handed out an illustrated program at the Hindu wedding written in English that explained each part of the Hindu ceremony for the non-Hindu guests in attendance. I expect that Peter translated that ceremony into Mandarin for his non-English speaking parents.

EXPLORING THEOLOGIES OF RELIGIONS

Raimundo Panikkar, a practicing Catholic priest, is a spiritually fluid person claiming connections to Catholic, Hindu, and Buddhist traditions.[1] He brings a unique understanding to theologies of religions that supports the reality that, in many cases, two religious traditions may inform and shape one another. This is helpful as we begin to see the transformative quality that interfaith religious engagement has on the couples. Panikkar speaks of a trans-global, trans-historical, trans-spiritual methodology that is helpful in our multireligious world. His essay "The Jordan, the Tiber, and the Ganges" is more than just a *study of God* that "theology" suggests; rather, in it, he articulates a methodology of understanding our diverse religious worlds in a sociopolitical landscape.[2] Panikkar introduces the idea that religions change over time through the complex relationships between the

1. Knitter, *Introducing Theologies of Religions*, 126.
2. Panikkar, "Jordan, the Tiber," 97.

history, tradition, location, and experiences of the particular believers in a particular epoch in human history. "Religions are not static constructs."[3] Christianity, and other religious traditions, are influenced by language, location, and culture, but also by epoch, geography, and history. Religious traditions change over time based on the layers of influence in a particular language-culture-place-time. Each adherent receives their religious meaning from their historical traditions, but then they are influenced by the era and conversations in which they are a part.[4] Epoch impacts Christianity as much as Christianity impacts any particular epoch. For example, the Christian Right is remaking Christianity in its white male image, while the #MeToo social movement is giving feminist theology new relevancy within the context of churches and congregations worldwide.

By taking the long view of religions over time, Panikkar recognizes the power of a people, place, and period to literally transform the faith in action of a particular religious tradition. He writes,

> Christian self-understanding has to be open to other religious experiences, and belief-forms (and systems), to be willing to listen to them, to learn from them, and even to incorporate anything that appears to enrich or deepen Christian interpretation, *to be ready for a mutual transformation.* This interreligious fertilization may produce a new awareness and even, eventually, a new form of religious consciousness or religion.[5]

Promoting both a self-reflective view of Christianity *and* a global-contextual understanding of the Christian experience within a larger religiopolitical world, Panikkar compels us to participate in a dialogical process that is not mere understanding, but, rather, is itself a dialogical enterprise. "The very agenda of the dialogue should be worked out in the dialogue itself."[6] Within the dialogue between the religious traditions, for example Hinduism and Christianity, the partners—let us say a Hindu philosopher and a Christian theologian—by cocreating religious meaning, determine their language and method of understanding. They thus create their unique meaning-making process and craft new theology together, rather than have one person (usually the more powerful, privileged person) setting the terms by which dialogue *should* happen without considering the *other* person. By

---

3. Panikkar, "Jordan, the Tiber," 92.
4. Panikkar, "Jordan, the Tiber," 96.
5. Panikkar, "Jordan, the Tiber," 97. Emphasis added.
6. Panikkar, "Jordan, the Tiber," 102.

doing so, not only do they create the foundations for their work together, but they also create something entirely new while attempting to avoid the elitism or colonialism often built into dialogical experiences that are generally hosted by Western white Christian male academics. According to Panikkar, "its decisions and insights can be momentous" highlighting the "creativity and freedom of authentic theologizing" that crosses traditions, culture, ethnicities, and geography.[7] Panikkar pushes us to recognize that Christianity has never been owned by any one people, any one epoch, or, in fact, any one religious tradition.

If we take Panikkar seriously, we understand that each religious tradition is influenced and transformed by encounters with others—in a particular epoch, a particular dialogical moment, or a particular geopolitical event. It is a global perspective toward understanding that a theology of religions itself must accommodate a spiritually fluid global religious movement able to define and redefine itself by the dialogical events in which it participates. People of faith must be able to accommodate how communities adapt their own practice of religious doctrine in their particular context, location, and period of history. Our faith traditions can grow and change over time. We can see this in some respects with the example of Peter's Taiwanese evangelical Christian perspective being reshaped toward more progressive values in light of his multicultural interfaith marriage. Over time and in new contexts, religious values and practices can be refashioned.

For example, while in seminary, I visited the United Theological Seminary of Bangalore in South India. There the librarian gave me a tour of the archives in the basement, where she showed me photos of the early professors and members of the Bangalore Christian Society. The first-generation photos were of all European ethnically white people. The second- and third-generation photos became more and more Indian in ethnicity until all the people in the photos were of Indian origin and there were no longer any Europeans in the photos. While the Christian heritage quickly became indigenous, it was not without the risk of also inheriting a colonial Christian theology. That then evolved further to become more religiously inclusive by the fact of living inside of a mostly Hindu culture.

---

7. Panikkar, "Jordan, the Tiber," 97.

MEASURING INTERFAITH RELIGIOUS ENGAGEMENT

How does one measure interfaith religious engagement within a multicultural interfaith marriage? This was a question I wanted to explore in my survey of couples from around the world. Religious engagement, as I defined it, included talking about God, faith, spirituality, or religion with their partner. It also involved attending religious ceremonies or services outside of the home, for example attending a church service or a special event at a synagogue. And the survey invited estimates regarding the amount of time spent in religious practices of prayer, meditation, or reading of scripture in the home. The survey results suggest that this group of individuals are more religiously engaged than most, with 62 percent of couples reporting that they "talk about faith/spirituality/God/religion" at least monthly with their partner. The person who filled out the survey reported on both their and their partner's engagement with daily, weekly, or monthly "spiritual practices, such as prayer/meditation/chanting or reading of a sacred text." The respondents' personal religious engagement was 59 percent in a spiritual practice at least monthly, with 42 percent reporting that their partners did the same on at least a monthly basis. With regards to weekly or monthly attendance of religious services, only 16 percent of the couples surveyed did so. Whereas, 33 percent performed a religious ritual in their home on a daily, weekly, or monthly basis. A big measure of interfaith religious engagement is whether the couple had a religious wedding ceremony or not, or if they actually hosted two religious ceremonies representing both of the couples' religious traditions. At least one religious wedding ceremony was conducted by 66 percent of the couples surveyed, with 34 percent reporting that they did not have a religious ceremony for their wedding. Of our couples 27 percent held two religious weddings or ceremonies. Those couples who had two religious wedding ceremonies, were engaged in conversations that crossed both of their religious traditions. They likely had those conversations with their partner's family, religious clergy or leader within both of their faith traditions.

DIALOGUE MEANS HAVING THE HARD CONVERSATIONS

Using a skill that is typical among multicultural interfaith couples, Adam and Maria from Costa Rica are willing to have the hard conversations.

Typically, interfaith dialogue is an academic exercise where people from different faith traditions engage in theological debate or share in experiences of encounter or culturally immersive events. These are educational and supportive of broadening the hearts and minds of people who come from vastly different traditions. Yet the commitment and investment are so much higher when their concern is the longevity of the marriage and the health and wellbeing of their children. The stakes are higher, the commitment to stay in the conversation is greater, and the willingness to confront the harsh realities of prejudices and stereotypes found within the partner's community is humbling. Adam and Maria were willing to face the authentic truth and work through their own beliefs and perspectives on a variety of issues that faced their relationship. Some of them included their perspectives on LGBTQ relationships, which, during their Catholic pre-marital counseling sessions, were not supported by the Roman Catholic Church. Adam realized that for him rights for LGBTQ people was a matter of justice and equality. So to understand one another's religious views better the two of them sat in the park after their sessions, for hours, and discussed this issue in some detail. In those conversations Maria appreciated Adam's perspective and the culture of inclusivity in which he was raised. She shared with him that there were things within the Catholic faith that she did not believe and this was an area of growth for her. Another of those hard conversations was about how Adam had changed his mind about raising their children within the Jewish faith, Maria talks of this shift directly to Adam, "In the beginning, you told me that you only cared about having the important holidays at the house, but then you changed your mind. You told me that you did want your kids to go to Jewish school and do a [bar mitzvah]. It was a long and hard conversation." A third example is how they will talk about who Jesus is from their respective traditions with their young son, who is being raised in both religions. In a remarkable conversation about Christology, Maria shares her own growth within her Catholic faith: "I believe in Jesus, that Jesus was the son of God, and that he came down to earth. But I think that there is a possibility that he wasn't the Messiah. I think that—I'm not sure—if someone else doesn't believe it, they could be right." They have taken the time to talk about who Jesus is from each of their religious perspectives and, ultimately, they are staying open and recognizing that each person is raised within a distinct religious tradition and culture. As a result of having these hard conversations across their religious traditions, they both report having grown in their respective faiths. For Adam, he indicates he is *more religious* than his parents because he is able to practice both religions within his home, whereas his parents, especially his mother, were not permitted that same flexibility or provided support. For Maria, she is more open to other world religions and their unique perspectives. When asked what benefit these hard conversations have had on her, she shares her own transformation, "Well for me, it's opened my mind, like, I've discovered, especially having grown up in a strict Catholic family, realizing that no one has the absolute truth about God, or about history, and that we're all the same, really. That I'm Catholic, in reality, because I was born into a Catholic family. If I were born into a Hindu family, I would be Hindu." Adam and Maria have worked to not only grow within themselves but also have, in the process, shared with others what a healthy happy truly multicultural interfaith family can look like. In the end, they could not possibly choose one culture, one language, or one religion over the other. They are all of those things—a Jewish American Costa Rican Catholic multicultural interfaith family. The lesson for those of us who are clergy in faith communities and leaders in institutions that serve young couples and families is that we have a choice we must make. Will we affirm or deny multicultural interfaith couples the *right to be who they are and to define, for themselves, which traditions are important? Will clergy and community leaders be barriers or advocates for multicultural interfaith couples?*

15

Talking about Faith, Activism, and the Religious Other

IN MY QUALITATIVE ANALYSIS of my survey data, I wanted to explore further the question of whether there was a correlation between the level of a couple's religious engagement and their social change agency in their communities. I was also curious if these survey results suggest that the amount of tension and conflict experienced in the relationship correlates with either the couple's level of religious engagement or the couple's amount of social change agency. To do this I needed to quantify the individual couple's responses to the eight questions measuring religious engagement, the eight questions measuring tension and conflict, and the eleven questions measuring social change agency. I devised a valuation score for each couple's answers to these twenty-seven questions, giving all fifty-six couples an RE score—an Interfaith Religious Engagement score; a TEN score—Tension and Conflict score; and an SC score—Social Change Agency score. These scores were on a one-hundred-point scale and they were plotted against each other. In all, three plots were created to see if there was a visible correlation between any of these measures. Among those surveyed, the data plots did not suggest a correlation between TEN and SC or TEN and RE. In other words, the tension and conflict a couple experienced as a result of their multicultural interfaith relationship seems to have no observable correlation with either their interfaith religious engagement or their social change agency and activities, with those couples surveyed. While my interviewed couples shared that their experience of tension and conflict, because of their multicultural

TALKING ABOUT FAITH, ACTIVISM, AND THE RELIGIOUS OTHER

interfaith relationships, did have an impact on their social change agency, this data, while not refuting that claim, did not support it. The survey may not be the appropriate place to ascertain the connections between the tension and conflict a couple experiences and their social change agency. Yet, the interview data does point to that conclusion.

What is remarkable is the question of a correlation between religious engagement and social change agency. When Interfaith Religions Engagement (RE) is plotted against Social Change Agency (SC), there does seem to be an observable positive correlation among the couples surveyed. See Figure 15.1. This chart shows how each couple's data points on the Interfaith Religious Engagement score, from one to one hundred, along the x-axis is charted against their Social Change Agency score along the y-axis. There seems to be a positive trend shown by a majority of the data points that lie within the two lines. While there are outliers from this trend, this figure would suggest that as (RE) Interfaith Religious Engagement increases in the life of a couple, so does their Social Change Agency (SC), as indicated by the multicultural interfaith couples represented in this sample. Thus, as RE increases, SC also tends to increase.

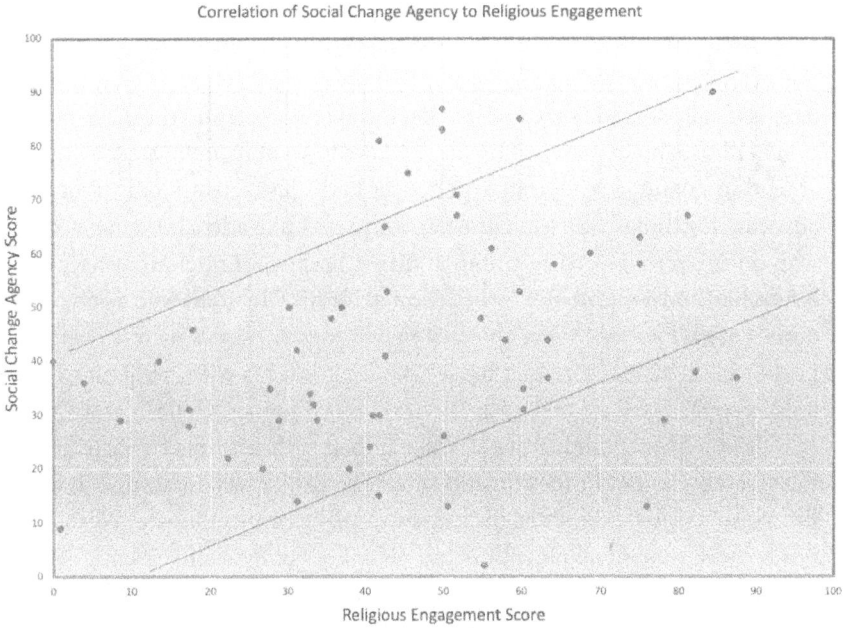

Figure 15.1 Correlation of Social Change Agency to Interfaith Religious Engagement

The implication for our communities and faith leaders might be to encourage our multicultural interfaith couples to talk more about their faith and the differences in their traditions with one another. Do not be afraid of religious differences. And perhaps, by extension, we can encourage ourselves to dig in deeper with people in our communities who are different than ourselves. These conversations could lead to positive social change. For those leaders who are committed to social justice and advocacy, one source of community participation and leadership could come from members who are part of a multicultural interfaith couple. They may have acquired skills for advocacy and care deeply about justice issues which arise from belonging in an intersectional family. A word of caution, however—this study is not a formal quantitative analysis. These are not concepts that can be measured using traditional standards so a positive correlation line one may see in other data sets would not apply here. In an attempt to look deeper into the relationship between religious engagement and social change agency, we can see that these two do seem to have some correlation among those surveyed. This is an encouraging result and warrants further investigation.

The amount of tension and conflict a couple experienced did tend to have an impact on Social Change Agency, as shown in the in-depth interviews data of our eight couples, yet was not evidenced in the data correlation. For example, our Catholic-Christian/Hindu-Atheist couple, Máire and A. S., specifically shared that experiencing racial prejudice, and the discrimination her husband experienced, caused Máire to want to advocate for others. "I tend to take A. S.'s internal experiences and I just scream and shout and advocate for things he's felt and dealt with. . . . I like advocating for people who don't have a voice." With our Indian Christian/Hindu-Atheist couple, Arundhati and Sanjaya, Sanjaya advocated for his Christian wife against the desires of his mother for her conversion. He does not shy away from helping people who need it or telling those who question his wife's religion to not judge people based on their religion or their economics. Colleen and Shiva, our UU-Buddhist/Hindu couple, who, among my interview subjects, faced the greatest conflict in their relationship, shared that when faced with conflict now, "We will take a step back and we will be compassionate. We will go respectfully about dealing with it, but we're not going to shrink back." Even in our youngest couple, who are in a Muslim/Sikh interfaith relationship, Kamalpreet and Kamran, their struggle for eight years to gain the approval of their parents has equipped them to advocate not only among their two families but also among their friends' parents, who have found their own children dating across religious traditions. Additionally, Kamran serves as a mentor to at-risk youth in his community to empower those who lack opportunities, and Kamalpreet cares a great deal for women reentering the workforce and organizes training for women's groups to do just that. From the interview data, then, it would seem that tension and conflict contribute toward couples learning the skills necessary to navigate social change within their communities. In all, qualitative in-depth interviews are capable of revealing more nuanced information from these intersectional couples than perhaps a survey could produce; yet both types of research are valuable for this kind of deeper dive into the lives and experiences of multicultural interfaith couples from around the world.

When we talk about interfaith dialogue and its benefits, it is important to note that many of the theologians advocating for this model contain inherent biases, which center Christianity as *the tradition* that is primary with *others* as secondary. Along with that notion is that within Christianity there is an embedded view that a theology of religions or interfaith dialogue presupposes that by being Christian one holds a superior or privileged perspective, in part, because of more voices coming from the Christian context, myself included. From this view then, what Christians suggest as the way to engage others may be construed as the best or, even, only way to engage other religious traditions. This may lead us to miss some important contributions from those who engage in interfaith dialogue and social change agency from religious traditions or worldviews such as Hinduism, Buddhism, atheism, Judaism, Islam, and Sikhism, as is shown by the diverse couples represented in the interviews discussed earlier. Further, when we center the Christian experience in our theologies of religions and interfaith dialogue, we may presume that people adhere to only one religious tradition. What we learn from these multicultural interfaith couples is that their religious practices, beliefs, and interfaith engagement may reflect a more spiritually fluid religious identity that is influenced, and, in some cases, transformed by their long-term engagement with their partner, who does not share the same religious affiliation.

My goals include developing an interfaith practical theology of social change that acknowledges how interfaith religious engagement in a multicultural relationship impacts the religious and cultural identity of both of the persons within the couple. Their faith, their beliefs, their perspectives will evolve and change over time as they dive deeper into their partner's culture and religious perspective. In short, multicultural interfaith couples are changed by their experiences with their partner and these changes not only impact their religious identity and cultural understandings but also shape their desire to *do something on behalf of others who face discrimination or prejudices based on religion, race, culture, or national origin.* To begin to articulate what an interfaith practical theology of social change might involve, we will look at the skills our couples acquire in their relationships, the ways in which they were agents for social change in their communities, and biblical examples of multicultural interfaith leadership. Finally, in the words of our interviewed couples, we will explore the kinds of leadership our world needs today.

RESPONDING TO THE RELIGIOUS OTHER

When we encounter someone who is racially, ethnically, culturally, or religiously different than ourselves, it is not uncommon to feel concerned or fearful, curious or hospitable. These are two distinct responses to someone who could be perceived as a threat to our person, our family, or our way of life. Will we work to insulate and protect our family and community against them? Or will we work to build new relationships and invite these people who have a different culture and religious worldview into our lives? Our responses are often based on inherited theologies about other religions within our own belief systems. These theologies of religions can be simplified into three primarily categories:

1. *Exclusivist*—our culture and religion are the best and right way to view the world. To the religiously and culturally othered person, the exclusivist might say, "You are not part of us. We do not trust you. You do not belong here." And they would seek their exclusion or demand their conversion.

2. *Inclusivist*—our culture and religion are not the only ones in the world, and we are curious and open to inviting others into our worldview. To the religious and culturally othered person, the inclusivist might say, "You are different than us, but you can be part of us. We will include you into our way of life."

3. *Pluralist*—the different cultures and religions of the world are distinct and unique. We want to learn more about other cultures and religions on their own terms. To the religious and culturally othered person, the

pluralist might say, "You are distinct, and your worldview is unique. Tell us more about what is important to you and how we can be a part of your life. We value you as you are."

Demian Wheeler joins theologians such as Paul Knitter, Marjorie Suchocki, and many others in articulating that interfaith dialogue and religious engagement are best suited when a theology of religions stands firmly within the pluralist viewpoint. Wheeler views "the pluralist model as the only viable option in the theology of religions," and he calls on "pluralists such as Hick and Knitter on the voyage across the religious Rubicon, imploring the faiths to relinquish any pretense of finality, absoluteness, universal normativity, and the like, and to accept, even welcome, 'the thoroughly pluralized character of human religious and cultural life.'"[1] The diversity of individual human experiences across race, culture, and religious difference plays an important role in our propensity or willingness to engage the religious other in our community. Some will be eager to engage others for the purposes of dialogue; others, however, will not. Is that necessarily a determining factor for growth or social change agency?

While the theologians mentioned here argue that the *pluralist* view is the preferred stance for a theology of religions, it is not necessary that the families of origin of our multicultural couples adopt that view for there to be fruitful religious engagement or social change agency within their families because of the interfaith marriage. Where you begin is not necessarily where you will end. As we learned from the experiences of the couples interviewed, the parents of the couples were not always curious or interested in engaging with their adult child's chosen partner. You might say they held an *exclusivist theology*, but over time their views of the religious other changed because of their love of their adult child and they began to practice a more *inclusivist theology* with their child's partner. There are a range of responses that are possible when parents encounter the culturally and religiously othered prospective sons-in-law or daughters-in-law; for our purposes, we shall call them *others-in-law*. Yet most of those responses will fall within two categories—the desire to protect the family or the desire to build new relationships with their future *other-in-law*. See Table 15.2.

---

1. See Wheeler, *Religion within the Limits*, 82.

Table 15.2 Possible Responses to the Religious Other-In-Law

Response to Religious Other-In-Law Insulate/Isolate/Protect	Response to Religious Other-In-Law Build Relationships
Brings out feelings of fear, anger, shame, and avoidance.	Brings out feelings of caution, concern, curiosity, and hospitality.
Protect my family/tribe/community from the outsider.	Begin a conversation based on mutuality and trust.
Prevent my child from dating/marrying the religious or culturally othered person.	Ask my child questions based on concerns and desire to learn more about their proposed partner.
Rely on stereotypes and existing prejudices about the other. Rely on existing knowledge and experiences.	Explore aspects of the culture, traditions, and practices of the other. Discover new things. Experience aspects of the other person's way of life.
Strategize ways to resist or fight the proposal.	Strategize ways to bridge the differences and find common ground.
Find good reasons why the relationship will fail.	Find evidence of similar relationships that have succeeded.
Seek allies who will advocate for your point of view.	Seek allies who will advocate for your point of view.
Find institutional support to prevent the marriage.	Find institutional support to bless the marriage and guide the couple.
Engage in conversations designed to block the relationship from continuing. Highlight the conflicts and tensions inherent in the culture or religious tradition.	Engage in conversations that encourage mutual sharing without avoiding the hard conversations. Take your time, keep engaging.
Strive to get your points across and prove your argument is valid.	Practice intentional compassionate listening. Engage in multicultural, interracial, and interfaith dialogue.
Values the purity of their culture, race, or religion and desires to protect and preserve the community and its culture, beliefs, and norms.	Values the diversity of the world's cultures, races, and religions. May see their own culture as an evolving tradition that has been impacted by many generations of diverse people's contributions.

Any family member, including the couples, may find themselves on either side or both sides of the table above. For instance, in my husband's family their initial reactions to me as their prospective *other-in-law* was to resist the proposal and to share the importance of their religious and cultural traditions with their son. As their son persisted in his desire to marry me, they shifted their actions to ones that were more inclusive and hospitable. Yet they were not so curious as to value my religious tradition or culture. They were willing to incorporate me into *their culture and traditions*. This would be consistent with moving from a more *exclusivist* theology of religions to an *inclusivist* theology of religions, as explained above. Another example would be Colleen and Shiva, our UU-Buddhist/Hindu couple. If you recall, Shiva's parents were opposed to the marriage and used many of the strategies above to prevent the relationship from moving forward. They sought allies within their religious community and with their astrologer, they wrote letters to Shiva's doctoral advisor and wrote a letter to Colleen's father trying to enlist him to prevent the marriage. If we locate their actions within the table, we can see that while they were challenging and, even to some extent, harmful, they were situated within a perspective that valued their family's culture, traditions, and religious perspectives. They desired to preserve their heritage for generations to come. There is a certain realism, then, to their argument not to marry across the cultures. When we engage in deep listening, we can appreciate that they do have the best interests of their son in mind.

A THEOLOGY BASED ON LOVE, DIGNITY, AND EQUITY

An interfaith practical theology of social change is built on the concepts of mutual love, the inherent dignity of human beings, and the desire for fair and equal treatment for all people. Love, dignity, and equity are at the heart of an interfaith practical theology of social change. Without the love of *the other*, there will be no need to challenge or, ultimately, change the community's views toward the culturally or religiously othered person. It is precisely because of the love of their proposed partner that they are willing to advocate for the inherent dignity and demand fair treatment of them with their family and community. Love drives the action. While I may not like how someone is treated in my community, I will not necessarily be committed to *do something about that unequal treatment* if I do not care deeply for them and their welfare, as would be the case of my partner or my child. Like Martin Luther King Jr.'s call for everyone's "somebodiness," the one who advocates for their partner with their parents is acting out their profound love and declaring that their partner is *somebody*. They are worthy of being in the family. They are worthy of being included. Finally, inclusion suggests that they would also invite the fair and equal treatment of their prospective partner, not just within the family, but with the institutions and community at large. When religious institutions refuse to marry multicultural interfaith couples, the religious adherent can request inclusion, suggest adaptations, or recommend policy changes that will allow for their chosen partner to be welcomed within their community. They can, in the process of advocating for the one they love, be social change agents for those couples who will follow in their footsteps. In cultures where the nondominant person is often discriminated against, it is the responsibility of the privileged member of the couple to engage in the advocacy work with the health care system, the school system for their children, as well as the religious institution. Advocacy extends toward personal relationships as well. For example, in a gathering of friends who do not speak their partner's language, they will need to translate the language that is spoken within the group to the language that their partner understands. They will need to explain the current contextual cultural expectations to their partner, but also translate the culture of their partner to their friends and community. Advocacy for their *religiously and culturally othered partner* invites advocacy conversations in everyday settings with friends, family, and institutions in order to go about the commitments of their everyday lives.

As these couples navigate worlds of difference between their cultures, languages, nationalities, and religious traditions, they will undoubtedly face resistance, stereotypes, and institutional discrimination. As they persist in sharing their love, standing for the dignity of their spouse, and insisting on fair treatment, those people and institutions that were resistant may begin to bend and change over time. Their views of *the other* may expand as they get to know *this person that is loved by another*. Their ideas about the *othered person* may shift, and curiosity may replace fear. Hospitality may replace the desire to protect the family from outsiders. Over time once-resistant parents may become strong advocates and allies for the *other-in-law*, going so far as to *adopt* their in-law as their claimed adult child. We see this in Usha and Patrick's relationship when, in India, in preparations for the Hindu wedding, Patrick is adopted as one of Usha's uncle's sons. They claim him as their fifth son, and, thus, he becomes one of *their Pandavas*, a scripture reference, which indicates a high level of inclusion of Patrick into the family. We see this with Arundhati and Sanjaya; after eight years, she begins to claim herself as a full member of her Hindu family. Later she is acknowledged by an elder in Sanjaya's family for playing a role in broadening the family's ability to be inclusive toward others. And in my own case, my deep love for my husband transferred to a deep love and appreciation for my own parents-in-law, which, in turn, led to their adopting me as their daughter. Having little connection and support from my own family of origin, their love was not only affirming, but it was also an identity-transforming experience because they said that I was *somebody* worth loving and they were willing to welcome me and make a place for my belonging within their family.

16

Newfound Leadership Skills

EACH OF THE MULTICULTURAL interfaith couples interviewed acquired leadership skills during the tenure of their relationship. Over the extended period within their relationship, our couples learned to navigate a variety of differences while experiencing tension, conflict, questions of belonging and legitimacy, prejudice, discrimination, and exclusion. There are some common skills that were demonstrated in our multicultural interfaith couples. A summary of those skills is listed in Table 16.1, "Leadership Skills Found in Multicultural Interfaith Couples," and will be discussed in some detail.

A common experience in many of our multicultural interfaith couples was their expanding ideas of identity and subsequent ability to encourage authenticity in others. Their own identity expanded to reflect their changing views around race, religion, or culture, and required a deepening sense of who they are in relationship to their partner and the diverse communities in which they lived. In the process they may have shared a new view of who they are with their family, a process of self-differentiation from the expectations of their parents or their community. We saw this skill demonstrated with A. S. as he prepared to share his relationship with Máire with his parents and their Gujarati community. He made a choice about which cultural identity he would own and how he would communicate this compassionately to his dad and family. Cathy, as she explored taking vows within the Buddhist community, went through what she called "a breaking open" of herself and her identity. She shed the limiting aspects of her former Catholic identity and found comfort and healing in the Buddhist practices of compassion. She, along with her husband Paul, then was able to witness the suffering and conflicts in El Salvador and create trusting long-lasting relationships that allowed them to return year after year.

This skill of *expanding ideas of identity and encouraging authenticity* creates an ability to generate both personal authenticity as well as invite others into deeper authentic expressions, which become an asset in building trust between communities that have a history of tension or conflict. Having grown in their own understanding of complex identities, they can encourage and invite others to share the intersectional aspects of their lives, encouraging authenticity and trust in relationships.

In the formation of their relationships, our couples had to navigate the differences in their cultural and religious traditions and, while doing so, they may have developed an *appreciation for cultural and religious difference*. Some of our couples organized two religious wedding ceremonies representing the customs and traditions of both religions and, in turn, honored both of their families. Doing this additional work introduced both sides of the family to the other faith tradition and required the partners to engage in hard conversations that may have included advocacy work with their religious-others-in-law. Maria and Adam, our Catholic/Jewish couple from Costa Rica, shared about the many cultural and religious encounters they shared with both sides of the family. From a Jewish baby-welcoming ceremony hosted by a progressive rabbi in the United States, to a Catholic priest offering to include the Jewish tallit in the marriage ceremony, this couple learned to appreciate their individual religious expressions and expose others to those traditions as well. Cathy and Paul knew and worked with diverse communities. They appreciated people from a variety of religious traditions, including Quaker, Buddhist, Christian, Catholic, and Hindu traditions. Máire and A. S. shared the religious traditions of their neighbors with their children whether they were Hindu, Muslim, or Jewish.

Our couples have also learned the skill of *adapting traditional practices to new circumstances* in the course of their relationships. For instance, Arundhati and Sanjaya did not desire to have a religious wedding and wanted to avoid the inevitable conflicts that religious weddings in India would bring. Instead, they had a civil wedding with a few of their friends present along with the judge. They adapted their plans to modify the reception following the civil wedding to include religious elements at the request of their mutual families. With the pressure of the traditional religious wedding rituals removed from their planning, the families were able to think more creatively about ways they could bless the couple, using elements from their own religious tradition. Each side called upon priests and other elders in the community to offer a prayer or blessing at the dinner and congratulatory toasts to the couple. Maria and Adam, in Costa Rica, could not find a *mohel* to perform the circumcision of their son. They adapted the tradition and separated the religious rituals from medical procedures out of necessity. Later, in the United States, they had a progressive rabbi perform a welcoming ceremony that awakened their son's senses to the new world around him.

Another skill that is often acquired is *navigating and translating culturally and religiously different spaces.* As othered persons learn to navigate, feel comfortable within, and belong to their partner's cultural or religious spaces, there is a significant change from being an outsider to belonging—a feeling of *"I belong here in both the Hindu temple and the Christian church."* To do so they must not only learn the customs and language, and dress appropriate to those spaces, but they must also be able to translate for their family members and friends who accompany them. In the process, our couples learned to teach others. They were able to translate for other outsiders and helped them navigate inside that culturally religious world with ease. For instance, I have led immersive experiences to our local Hindu temple for many friends and family. Beyond that, I have been invited to take future Christian clergy, still in seminary, to these spaces and teach them about Hindu practices in these places of worship with the support and blessing of the local Hindu priests. I also had the endorsement of my *appa*—who is my Hindu father-in-law and an expert in South Indian Iyengar Hindu religious practice. Máire and A. S., a Catholic-Christian/Hindu-Atheist couple, learned to navigate Catholic and Episcopal places of worship as they raise their two boys within the Christian tradition. Máire learned the customs and practices within the tight-knit Gujarati community in South Carolina and was able to navigate those spaces with ease. She was able to do this to such an extent that she advocated for her Indian coworker when that coworker faced difficulties in her Hindu marriage.

It is an essential skill of communication in multicultural interfaith couples to learn the art of *deep listening to underlying commitments.* Learning to listen to one another, to imagine what the commitments are behind what people are saying, even if what they are saying is hurtful, is what I mean by *deep listening.* This skill requires patience and time and an ability to be comfortable in one's own identity. For instance, Colleen and Shiva faced a great deal of resistance to their relationship from both of their families. Yet to hear them speak about their families, they were able to easily communicate the commitment of Colleen's father to protect his daughter or Shiva's parents' desire to do what was best for their son. Colleen and Shiva listened deeply to what their parents were saying underneath their disapproval, disappointment, or prejudicial statements. We saw this kind of deep listening in Kamalpreet and Kamran, our Muslim and Sikh couple, when Kamran talked about the journey his mother endured when leaving India for East Pakistan and then the arduous journey to West Pakistan when, upon their arrival, her mother died. She ultimately immigrated to the United States. Kamran not only appreciated the hardship his mother faced, but he understood her resistance to his interfaith relationship. He knew the fear and concern she had about non-Muslims, including his fiancée, is a result of the religious violence she personally encountered.

Every couple I interviewed talked about the allies that helped them to navigate the difficulties in their relationship. Multicultural interfaith couples develop the skill of *finding allies to support them navigating conflict in their relationships*. Cathy and Paul, our Buddhist/Buddhist-Catholic couple, shared about a significant Jesuit priest, who supported them throughout the annulment tribunal. Usha and Patrick found allies in Patrick's grandmother, who, while not very religious herself, advocated for her son's Catholic faith within their newly forming family. Máire, married to A. S., found an ally in A. S.'s mother because of their shared understanding of being married to atheists. They both advocate for each other's religious identities even though Máire is Catholic-Christian and her mother-in-law is Hindu. Finding allies who support their multicultural interfaith relationship is very important for the stability and longevity of the relationship and is a skill that is useful for building networks of support for social change.

The next three skills I discuss are related to each other: *practicing patience over time; persevering during conflict;* and *having the hard conversations*. Our couples demonstrated the ability to be patient as they experienced resistance to their chosen partner. Kamalpreet and Kamran took eight years to achieve both of their parents' blessings for their interfaith relationship before their recent engagement. Usha and Patrick waited two years while they talked and listened to Usha's mother's concerns about their multicultural international interfaith relationship. Colleen and Shiva practiced a great deal of perseverance during conflict, particularly with Shiva's parents, even as they felt ashamed and hid their son's marriage from their friends in India for many years. Eventually Shiva's parents began to participate in the life of the family and, now, regularly visit one another in both countries and both homes, where everyone is welcome—including Colleen, who is welcomed in India as Shiva's wife. This is remarkable. Cathy and Paul learned to persevere as they witnessed the extreme suffering of the Salvadoran people during their violent conflicts in El Salvador. In fact, their perseverance took them back year after year to continue their advocacy and support of those communities. Maria and Adam spoke at length about the many hard conversations they had about their cultural, religious, and national differences. They talked about their differing views on gay rights, raising their children in both religious traditions, and their commitment to travel back and forth between the two countries so they can raise their son in both cultures, religions, and languages. Kamalpreet and Kamran had begun to have the hard conversations with their families and with each other as they found new ways of respecting and honoring one another's faith traditions while finding the common connections in the cultural traditions their families share. The skills to practice patience, persevere during conflict, and have the hard conversations without shrinking back are important skills for leadership and social change agency.

The final leadership skill is *developing compassionate responses* to complex and, often, controversial situations. By listening to the perspective of their partner or taking the time to understand their viewpoint of their family or religious institution, multicultural interfaith couples can see complex issues from multiple vantage points and respond in authentic, innovative, and compassionate ways. Paul and Cathy sought compassionate solutions to the complex geopolitical situations in El Salvador. Sanjaya, a peace activist, married to Arundhati in India, worked to broker peaceful solutions in religious tensions between Hindus and Christians in a northeastern state of India. A. S., married to Máire, "stood up for the little guy" when he invited a homeless man to dine with him and his sons. His wife Máire, having understood the complex nature of the intersection of race and poverty, worked as a "Low-Income Shopper Advocate," seeing that the needs of families with limited resources were underrepresented in advertising and product availability in larger retail chain stores. Kamalpreet, engaged to Kamran, organized women's empowerment groups designed to support women moving from raising children at home to reentering the workforce. These are compassionate solutions to complex situations we find within our communities.

Newfound Leadership Skills

Table 16.1 Leadership Skills Found in Multicultural Interfaith Couples

Leadership Skill	How It Can Be Applied
expanding ideas of identity and encouraging authenticity	Having grown in their own understanding of complex identities, they can encourage and invite others to share the intersectional aspects of their lives encouraging authenticity and trust in relationships.
appreciating cultural and religious difference	Beginning with navigating the cultural and religious differences in their couple, to planning their weddings, and hosting others, they can appreciate cultural and religious differences beyond their own.
adapting traditional practices to new circumstances	Discovering that traditional ceremonies or practices do not make room for their partner, family, or context, they learn to adapt and negotiate new ways of achieving the original goal in their context.
navigating and translating culturally and religiously different spaces	Having traveled between two different kinds of religious places of worship, and by being exposed to and learning to move freely inside, they act as ambassadors for others in distinct cultural settings.
deep listening to underlying commitments	Given their profound love of their partner and extraordinary commitment to making it work with their in-laws, they are able to listen to people who are different than themselves and seek common ground.
finding allies to support them navigating conflict in their relationships	Recognizing others in their community supported the formation of their relationship, they know the power of allied partnership and seek out people who have shared values and visions aligned with their goals.
practicing patience over time	Through the experience of talking with parents and in-laws, often over extended periods of time, they have learned the importance of patience in achieving goals that are complex and require nuanced solutions.
persevering during conflict	Through the reality of experiencing conflict between cultures or religions within diverse communities, they have learned that perseverance produces respect and may open new opportunities for growth and acceptance.
having the hard conversations	Not shying away from the difficult conversations within their relationship affords them the ability to step into challenging situations and broker solutions that would not have otherwise been possible.
developing compassionate responses	By listening to the perspective of their partner or their community viewpoint, they can see complex issues from multiple vantage points and respond in authentic, innovative, and compassionate ways.

Interfaith dialogue speaks of the importance of finding common ground and seeking similarities. Yet, multicultural interfaith couples have to go further in the kind and quality of the conversations that they are having because their conversations are often complex and emotionally charged; even more, they involve matters of their identity, religious belonging, and cultural longevity. Their conversations are intersectional in nature and of vital importance to themselves and their communities. In other words, there is more at stake and more to risk if they fail. Belonging to a family, culture, and community can be a matter of survival. Remaining an outcast within a community can be damaging, isolating, and, ultimately, will not serve our goals of positive social change for diverse communities. These ten skills, forged in the fires of their multicultural interfaith relationships, are effective tools for leaders who desire to work for social change within their larger community contexts.

TYPES OF SOCIAL CHANGE AGENCY

Our multicultural couples engaged in a variety of social change activities. Their agency ranged from catalyzing change within their families to their religious communities to making changes within their workplaces and larger social contexts. The ways they were able to affect change depended on which leadership skills they were able to employ in their context and circumstances. Dr. Steve Newcom from the Kaleo Center has created the "Eightfold Dimensions and Dynamics of Social Transformation."[1] In this handout he highlights the importance of the categories of *encounter, proclaim, envision, organize, advocate, and educate* to provide for social transformation. There is some overlap between the categories above and the types of social change agency observed in the Multicultural Interfaith Couples interviewed. Based on qualitative analysis of those transcribed interviews, the variety of observed categories of social change can be seen in Table 16.2, "Types of Social Change Agency Observed in Multicultural Interfaith Couples," on the following pages.

What is an agent of social change within the context of multicultural interfaith couples? This is a person who, by their actions, cause positive changes in their community with regards to perceived understandings about race, culture, religion, or national origin. They use their own skills and experiences to help others grow in their multifaith religious literacy

1. Newcom, "Sevenfold."

or cross-cultural competencies. They are patient and compassionate leaders, advocating, educating, engaging, hosting, and participating in a variety of events and activities that showcases the diversity of their family. They are catalysts for change. Their presence may spark reactions, invite conversations, stir up questions of curiosity, and propel others to grow in their religious sensitivity and cultural literacy. They may expose and remove stereotypes, reveal prejudices, and build kinder, more inclusive relationships, or, still, they may uncover discriminatory ways the dominant culture treats those who are marginalized, all the while building bridges between those same cultures.

These social change agents are willing to use their lives and their relationships as models for others to learn and grow in their inclusive understanding of what is possible in loving, open, and diverse relationships. For example, with our couple from India, Sanjaya, in his human rights activism, would be involved in the social change agency work of *evaluation* and *negotiation* as he worked on teams to create new policies around disarmament and development. Whereas his wife, Arundhati, as a seminary professor, would be involved in the social change agency work of *education* and *engagement*. Or consider our newly engaged couple. Kamran, by envisioning and developing a new digital phone application to track police incidents for the Black Lives Matter movement, would be engaged in the social change agency work of *leading, evaluating,* and *advocating*. His fiancée, Kamalpreet, with her work forming women's support groups, would be *educating* and *advocating*. Further still, our Catholic/Jewish couple in Costa Rica, Maria and Adam, were often involved in the work of *exposure* and *education* of others given that Adam was often the *only Jewish person* in his community. Additionally, our couple from the Midwest, Usha and Patrick, worked together as social change agents by *hosting, exposing,* planning *encounters,* and leading *immersive* experiences. Máire, married to A. S., makes it a point in her social change agency to *advocate* for the "voiceless" and *participate* in rallies and marches as well. Each of our interviewed multicultural interfaith couples were involved in more than one type of social change agency positively impacting their families and larger communities. These couples may not necessarily view themselves as social change agents, yet they are showing leadership by living and working inside of a community where their appearance, clothes, beliefs, or practices are not the norm. They become leaders of successful multicultural interfaith dialogue and engagement opportunities in their everyday lives by simply living, working, and sharing life together with people who do not belong to their culture or tradition.

Table 16.2 Types of Social Change Agency Observed in Multicultural Interfaith Couples

Advocate	Stand up, speak out, or step in. They may advocate for their partner initially, but, often, this leads to advocating on behalf of others in their community.
Educate	Teach others about their culture, norms, values, and religion informally in their communities or, more formally, within institutions of higher education. This may take the form of mentoring others as well.
Encounter	A shared conversation or experience with someone from a different culture or religion in a cultural context, such as a temple, market, or someone's home. It is more than mere exposure, but less than an immersion experience.
Engage	A willingness to engage in interfaith or cross-cultural dialogue by inviting question and answer sessions, as well as sharing experiences, beliefs, and resources with people from other cultures and traditions.
Evaluate	By examining institutional policies and structures, they can implement changes by evaluating the ways in which existing policies discriminate against people of certain races, cultures, or religious traditions.
Expose	In some cases, they may be the first person of their culture, race, or religion that the surrounding community has experienced. To expose others means to give them a view of someone who is different.
Host	Organize dinners in their homes or larger community events where they are able to include a wide variety of people. These experiences show the ways that hospitality can begin to change the hearts and minds of people.
Immerse	This is the most complex of activities and promotes transformative experiences across culture and religion. Opportunities to live inside of the community and be immersed in all aspects of the *othered culture* from food, to language, to traditions, builds multifaith literacy and cultural competency.
Lead	Some of our couples may be leaders in their community through their public speaking, directing programs or projects, or organizing larger community events that cross cultures and include diverse faith traditions.
Negotiate	A few of our couples were engaged in negotiations that bridged the differences between cultures or religious traditions during times of tension or conflict. This is a specialized kind of agency that utilizes many skills.
Participate	A willingness to "show up" at marches, rallies, protests, campaigns, and other public events. Participating in social movements is a type of agency.

17

Seeing Interfaith Leaders in Scripture

MOST OF OUR RELIGIOUS traditions have holy books or scriptures that help guide and shape our religious traditions. The stories within those scriptures may contain characters that will offer new insights into the blessings that couples from different religious traditions, cultures, languages, and races may bring. As a Christian minister by profession, I am trained to read and interpret the stories found within the Christian Bible, which includes stories shared with the Jewish tradition from the Hebrew portion of the Bible. What follows is a deeper look at three figures within my religious tradition whose leadership can be seen from a new perspective when we consider their interfaith relationships. These examples are meant to be demonstrative. There is an opportunity to seek new readings and interpretations from the variety of scriptures from our multiple traditions that shed new light on the positive impact multicultural interfaith couples may have had on our religious traditions but have been overlooked.

MOSES AS AN INTERFAITH CHILD AND A MULTICULTURAL INTERFAITH LEADER

Our interfaith practical theology of social change can be applied to at least three leaders found within the Judeo-Christian biblical texts. We will briefly explore the leadership of Moses, Ruth, and Esther as examples of leaders of social change in their communities who were married to people from different cultural and religious traditions. This is not an attempt at academic exegetical work on the biblical texts nor the particulars of all their accomplishments of leadership. Rather, we will briefly explore the ways that their relationships are multicultural interfaith marriages, and that their gifts of leadership may, in part, arise from the skills and social change agency gained from their marriage to someone who is *religiously and culturally othered.*

Moses was born in Egypt during a time of the oppressive rule of Pharaoh the king, who ordered the midwives to kill all the boys born to the Israelite women.[1] Moses' life was preserved by his Hebrew (Israelite) mother, who hid him from the Egyptians for three months. The Scripture uses the terms Israelite and Hebrew to refer to the culture and religion of the people who worship YHWH, the God of Abraham, Isaac, and Jacob. We come to understand that the Egyptians worship multiple gods who are depicted as images or idols of human or animal forms and they do not worship YHWH. To protect her son, Moses' mother puts him in a basket and sends him downriver, with his sister Miriam watching over the baby from a distance. Pharaoh's daughter sees the basket and Moses is retrieved by her maid. Miriam offers to assist the daughter of Pharaoh in her new role as mother and provide her with a wet nurse, who, consequently, is his birth mother. Moses, then, is raised by two mothers, his adopted mother and his birth mother—one who was culturally and religiously Egyptian and the other who is culturally and religiously Hebrew, one who is rich and powerful and the other who is poor, enslaved, and without power. Moses, then, by virtue of being raised in both cultures, is an *interfaith child* and a product of two cultures, two religions, two languages, and, certainly, two different economic castes of people—those who rule and those who are ruled.

Scripture says, "When the child grew up, she brought him to Pharaoh's daughter, and she took him as her son"[2] and presumably gave him a new Egyptian name—the name, we learn, is Moses. We do not know the name his Hebrew mother gave him or how old Moses was when he was transferred from the hands of his Hebrew mother into the hands of his Egyptian mother, but it is conceivable that he could have been as old as four or five when weaning would have been completed and he was able to toilet himself. Scripture does demonstrate that Moses is aware of his bicultural dual-faith status and the tension that arises within his identity when he sees "his people" and witnesses the injustice of "one of his own people"

1. Exod 1:16.
2. Exod 2:10.

being beaten by an Egyptian.³ He responds to this injustice by killing the Egyptian and hiding his body "in the sand." Then, when he scolded two of his Hebrew "people," who were "fighting," saying, "Why do you strike your fellow Hebrew?" they respond by confronting him with his murder of the Egyptian and rejecting his Egyptian authority over them when they say, "Who made *you* a ruler and judge *over us*?"⁴ They do not accept *him as their people*, rather they view him as among those who rule over them. Moses' dual identities are in conflict and he no longer belongs among the Hebrew people, with whom he sees kinship, nor among his adopted Egyptian culture and religion that are his family.⁵ And so, he flees to "the land of Midian,"⁶ where he will meet another people of, yet, a third distinct culture and other religious practices.

It is important to note that the Midianites *are not Israelites*. These are shepherds who are nomadic. According to Wilda Gafney in *Womanist Midrash*, "the foreign Midianites are not 'pagan' Canaanites; they worshiped God of the Holy Name, YHWH, on the mountain before Israel did, and their priest Jethro instructed Moses in the ways of serving their shared God."⁷ There Jethro the Midianite, his future father-in-law, rewards Moses for helping his daughters water his flock at the well and "he gave Moses his daughter Zipporah in marriage," who bore him a son. Moses names this son "Gershom" because he says, "I have been an alien residing in a foreign land."⁸ He is an "alien" or othered person, an outsider who was welcomed and given a wife, a home, and an occupation, saving him from the wrath of Pharaoh, who "sought to kill" him.⁹ Moses is now a product of three cultures and two distinct religious traditions, and has learned new ways of worshiping the Holy One from the *foreign* Midianites, before he returns to Egypt to face Pharaoh as the representative leader who is called to free the Israelite people.

---

3. Exod 2:11–12.

4. Exod 2:13–14. Emphasis mine.

5. In the NRSV Anglicized Edition the term used is "kinsfolk" rather than "people" in the NRSVUE. Both words connote for us a powerful understanding of Moses seeking belonging in an ethnic group with whom he has not yet found kinship. He is seeking entre, but is not granted it.

6. Exod 2:15.

7. Gafney, *Womanist Midrash*, 147.

8. Exod 2:21–22.

9. Exod 2:15.

As clergy and faith leaders, we rarely read our scriptural texts for clues about race, religious difference, and cultural distinctiveness. In seminary, while we are taught to contextualize the scriptural stories in the time and periods in which they are written, we do not view them from the perspective of national identities, cultural practices, racial distinctions, or religious diversity, except when that difference is an example of the *othered people whom we should shun, oppose, convert, or with whom we shall broker either war or peace*. Moses will work to broker a deal with Pharaoh over the release of his free laborers—enslaved laborers.

Moses must work to liberate the enslaved Israelite people from the privileged ruling class of Egyptian people by using the skills he learned from the nomadic free Midianite people. Referring back to Table 16.1, "Leadership Skills Found in Multicultural Interfaith Couples," we can see that Moses possesses several of these skill sets. Moses demonstrates an ability to *appreciate cultural and religious differences* as he can navigate between the three cultural worlds of Israel, Midian, and Egypt. He must *navigate and translate these different spaces* while *adapting the traditional practices*, what he has learned from Jethro and from YHWH in Midian to the Egyptian Pharaoh's palace. We see Moses' ability to *persevere during conflict* while *having the hard conversations* and *practicing patience* throughout the ten plagues, until the Israelites are freed from the clasp of Pharaoh's hand. Now applying what we have learned from Table 16.2, "Types of Social Change Agency Observed in Multicultural Interfaith Couples," we can say that, in his social change agency, Moses was an *advocate, engaged* Pharaoh, *hosted* community gatherings of the Israelite people, *immersed* himself and the Israelites in the Midianite culture and religious practices at Mount Horeb, as well as *negotiated*, and, without a doubt, *led* his people to the promised land. Moses can be seen as an interfaith social change agent and a biblical example for our interfaith practical theology of social change.

RUTH AS A MULTICULTURAL INTERFAITH SOCIAL CHANGE AGENT

Our second example of multicultural interfaith leadership within the biblical text lies with the complicated character of Ruth, from the biblical book of the same name. She is often referred to as "Ruth the Moabite" categorizing her immediately in the listener's ear as *othered, foreign,* or *an outsider*. Ruth is the widowed Moabite daughter-in-law of Israelite immigrants from

Seeing Interfaith Leaders in Scripture

Bethlehem, Naomi and her husband, Elimelech, who left their home to go to Moab because of a famine. After Naomi's husband and both her sons die, she begins the journey to return to Bethlehem, presumably to die herself. Imagining that this journey took place on foot, we are reminded of the many refugees who are forced to flee their lands because of war or famine or political strife. Many do not survive their perilous journeys. Naomi has no ability to care for herself—with no sons and no husband, she may not even survive the journey back home. Ruth must know this and likely worries for her safety. Naomi tells her daughters-in-law, Orpah and Ruth, "Go back each of you to your mother's house."[10] Refusing to leave her mother-in-law, Ruth delivers the most famous lines of fidelity, which are often interpreted as her conversion to Judaism, "Where you go, I will go; where you lodge, I will lodge; your people shall be my people, and your God my God."[11] She does not abandon Naomi, but, instead, accompanies her to Bethlehem, where she begins to make a way for them to survive by gleaning in the fields during the barely harvest.[12]

Ruth's resourcefulness and willingness to use the Hebrew laws that protected the rites of aliens and widows to glean behind the harvesters allows her to provide for herself and her mother-in-law when women were not given property or status to provide for their own economic security. Meeting Naomi's kin Boaz, who is an Israelite, and gaining his favor while gleaning in his field, Ruth heeds his advice to "keep close to my young women" and receives his promise of protection "I have ordered the young men not to bother you."[13] Bringing home an abundance of grain, "an ephah of barley," and ensuring their survival, Ruth the Moabite gives new hope and life to Naomi the Israelite, who had all but given up. Naomi, having her own identity crisis, starts calling herself *Mara* or "bitterness" rather than "sweetness," which her name, Naomi, means.[14] Subsequently, Naomi and her Moabite daughter-in-law Ruth devise a plan involving Ruth going to the threshing floor in the middle of the night, where Boaz sleeps after an evening of celebrating the harvest. Naomi instructs Ruth to "uncover his feet."[15] Uncovering his feet is a euphemism referring to the uncovering of his

10. Ruth 1:8.
11. Ruth 1:16.
12. Ruth 2:2–3.
13. Ruth 2:8–9.
14. Ruth 2:14–23.
15. Ruth 3:4.

genitalia to force her distant relative Boaz to act quickly. Boaz is startled by Ruth's presence in the middle of the night and is asked to "redeem" Naomi's husband, Elimelech's, land from the "next of kin," who has the first "right of redemption."[16] That is, the next of kin, who is male, has the right to buy the land first. Boaz has the second right. During their midnight encounter, Ruth asks Boaz to "spread your cloak over your servant,"[17] which involves his duty to not only buy the land, but also to care for both Naomi and Ruth. Moreover, it is the role of the redeemer to take Ruth as his wife and provide an heir for the line of Elimelech, Naomi's dead husband, who died along with his two sons. Boaz does all this and marries Ruth. The "Lord made her conceive, and she bore a son,"[18] who became the grandfather of King David. Ruth is named in the lineage of both King David and the lineage of Jesus, as seen in the Gospel of Matthew.[19] Ruth is proclaimed, by the women of Bethlehem, "your daughter-in-law, who loves you, . . . is more to you than seven sons."[20]

Amy-Jill Levine, in her commentary on Ruth, describes the complexity within the biblical text surrounding both the character of Ruth and her Moabite heritage. Moabites are unwelcome among the people of Israel; they are gentiles and their women become associated with hypersexualized views of non-Israelite women: "Moab is associated with hostility and with sexual perversity."[21] Further, Levine suggests that "Ruth's Gentile background remains as stigma"[22] despite the fact that "through her loyalty, fortitude, and cleverness, she secures the future for herself, for her mother-in-law, and for the Davidic line."[23] Rather than Ruth being valued for her culture and religion, which is different from Naomi's Jewish faith, her cultural heritage is treated in a stereotypical manner as one that she must shed through conversion. Ruth is considered the exception against other Moabite women because she is believed to have converted and becomes the wife and mother to the heir to the throne of David. Yet Gafney, in *Womanist Midrash*, reinterprets the traditional interpretation of Moabite women

16. Ruth 4:6.
17. Ruth 3:9.
18. Ruth 4:13.
19. Matt 1:5.
20. Ruth 4:15.
21. Levine, "Ruth," 85.
22. Levine, "Ruth," 84.
23. Levine, "Ruth," 84.

as being despised or avoided and claims them as "protowomanists."[24] She speaks of the religious practices of the people of Moab within the biblical text of Num 25, where the "Moabite women" invite the Israelites "to participate in their religious rituals," which may have included "queer" sexualized encounters between Israelite men and Moabite women as well as Israelite women with Moabite women.[25] The people of Moab worshiped multiple gods, who are referred to in the translated Hebrew as "the women's gods,"[26] though we do not know who these gods are by name. Gafney explains that we do learn of the name of one of the gods called "Ba'al of Peor," which means "simply Lord/Master of Peor,"[27] over the region of Moab. They are women-centered and rely on one another. Gafney suggests that the Israelite and Moabite women, "who are intimately involved . . . represent a type of womanist community."[28] She further points out that "Naomi tells the Moabite women Ruth and Orpah to go back home to Moab . . . to their 'mothers' households' describing Moabite culture in matrilineal terms."[29] With these concepts in mind, one questions whether Ruth *converted* or if a better way to describe her religious affiliation is that she is *spiritually fluid*, having belonging in two cultures and religious traditions—worshiping both her Moab homeland God "Ba'al of Peor" and the God YHWH of Israel, and valuing those traditions. Ruth values the company of women, the care and safety of her mother-in-law, and she centers her experiences around the women in the field and the town. This would be consistent with not only a womanist interpretation of the text, but also of an interfaith practical theology of social change.

What leadership skills found in multicultural interfaith couples (Table 16.1) apply to Ruth? Ruth understands an *expanding idea of identity and encourages authenticity* with her mother-in-law as she, by her presence, invites Naomi to see beyond her bitterness and her identity as "Mara" and envision a new hopeful future. Ruth is able to *navigate and translate* inside of these *culturally and religiously different spaces* by learning the legal rites of the foreign alien in the land. In this reading she is a dispossessed immigrant farmworker without status, who risks her safety to feed her family.

24. Gafney, *Womanist Midrash*, 141.
25. Gafney, *Womanist Midrash*, 138.
26. Gafney, *Womanist Midrash*, 140.
27. Gafney, *Womanist Midrash*, 140.
28. Gafney, *Womanist Midrash*, 141.
29. Gafney, *Womanist Midrash*, 141.

Ruth uses her own agency in *finding allies to support* her *navigating conflict in her relationships*—her status as an alien puts her at odds with the community. Her safety is in question; she has no one to protect her. She finds allies in Naomi, Boaz, the women in the field, and, ultimately, the women of the community. Finally, Ruth *develops compassionate responses* to the people in her life—to Naomi, and even to Boaz as she serves as a partner and model wife to such an extent that she is named in lineages of two kings within the world's religions of Judaism and Christianity. With her actions, Ruth *advocates* for her mother-in-law; *engages* with the other farmworkers of Bethlehem; *exposes* the locals to a *real Moabite woman*, not one who fits the stereotypes; and she, along with her mother-in-law, helps Boaz to *negotiate* a solution in an especially difficult legal situation of land ownership and the responsibility of providing a lineage for her dead husband. Ruth can be seen as a multicultural interfaith leader and a social change agent for women, whose ingenuity and resourcefulness provide for the survival of their family and transform what was considered a status and identity filled with shame into one that is regarded with pride and given a place of honor within two religious communities.

ESTHER AND GLEANING OTHER SCRIPTURAL MULTICULTURAL INTERFAITH SOCIAL CHANGE AGENTS

The two biblical characters discussed on the previous pages are not the only multicultural interfaith leaders in the Hebrew Bible. We could examine the multicultural interfaith marriage of Queen Esther, whose name and identity were changed from her Jewish name, Hadassah, to her Persian name, Esther, when she was taken by King Ahasuerus, in an arranged marriage, to be his new queen. She had to adapt to the Persian king's royal court and learn the practices and policies of their world from the court eunuchs. The book of Esther, which does not mention the name of God or describe any religious traditions or rituals other than fasting, could be a signal to faith leaders that there may be examples within our biblical texts that mirror our current climate of people who are *spiritual but not religious* within our own communities. We also learn, at her uncle's urging, that Esther must intentionally keep her Jewish heritage and identity hidden, suggesting that Esther had to forgo her culture and heritage and had to *pass as Persian* in her new home. When an edict for the annihilation of the Jews threatens her own survival, supported by her Uncle Mordecai, and attended by her many eunuchs, Esther risks her life to reveal to her husband and king her authentic cultural and religious identity. Queen Esther ultimately *leads, educates, evaluates* and *negotiates* a solution that will save her family and the lives of all Jewish people in the entire Persian empire, which spans, according to Scripture, from "India to Ethiopia."[30]

There are more examples of multicultural interfaith social change agents in our religious traditions if we will look for them. Perhaps we can take a lesson from Ruth, who gleans the fields to support her family, that it may be time for religious leaders to glean our own scriptural texts for stories that bring to life positive examples of multicultural interfaith marriages. Whether these texts come from Buddhist, Hindu, Islamic, Sikh, or other religious traditions, we may find sacred stories that tell of when strangers, outsiders, outcasts, or foreigners were welcomed or married who subsequently brought honor and pride to their new culture and people. Our faith traditions tend to readily find examples of xenophobic stereotypical tropes of outsiders threatening the lives and livelihoods of a people and disrupting their culture and religious practices. Instead, may we lift up those social change agents from within our religious traditions that exemplify the values of inclusion, compassion, innovation, adaptation, and advocacy. I believe there are many overlooked narratives of powerful men and women in our religious traditions whose leadership has made our faith richer and stronger because of their courageous contributions and the skills they bring from their multicultural interfaith relationships. Characters like Moses, Ruth, and Esther have provided visionary leadership, innovative solutions, as well as positive social change within our religious communities. One wonders what other characters in our faithful lives might emerge once we look for them?

---

30. Esth 1:1; 8:9.

18

Love, Dignity, Equity, and Duty

As we reflect on what we have learned from our fifty-six surveyed couples and the lives of our eight interviewed couples, as well as the examination of three biblical multicultural interfaith characters, an interfaith practical theology of social change is beginning to emerge. First and foremost, interfaith practical theology of social change is built on the foundation of *love.* Because of the profound love and acceptance that is found between people of different cultures and faiths who dare to love in spite of or, perhaps, *because of* their differences, they have a strong impetus for working through conflicts or tensions that divide peoples of different cultures or religions. Within these relationships, people from cultures and religions that are distinct and, often, at odds with one another may come to a new place of peace and collaboration. Some would go so far as to say that Love is the Higher Power, love is that transcendent quality that binds us together and calls us to love those whom we fear or even hate. The first letter of John says it best:

> Beloved, let us love one another, because love is from God; everyone who loves is born of God and knows God. Whoever does not love does not know God, for God is love.
>
> God is love, and those who abide in love abide in God, and God abides in them. There is no fear in love, but perfect love casts out fear; for fear has to do with punishment, and whoever fears has not reached perfection in love. We love because he first loved us. Those who say, "I love God," and hate their brothers or sisters, are liars; for those who do not love a brother or sister whom they have seen, cannot love God whom they have not seen. The

Love, Dignity, Equity, and Duty

commandment we have from him is this: those who love God must love their brothers and sisters also.[1]

Those with whom we have conflicts and tensions because of differences in culture, religion, race, class, caste, or national origin, who are our brothers, sisters, and siblings, may be inviting us into deeper relationships so that we might reach perfection in love. One possible avenue toward this "perfect love that casts out fear" may be achieved through the love of *the other, the feared, the hated, or the despised*. If we can love *them*, then they are no longer feared as outsiders, but become a member of our family, which is a part of God's larger human family. You might say they move from the status of being feared out-laws to that of being our in-laws.

This is a theme of salvation—for it is the transforming power through our *love of the stranger* that redeems us of our own privilege, xenophobic views, and broadens our understanding and idea of who God is and God's desire for beneficial human relationships across cultures, classes, *and religious differences*. Jesus speaks to this salvific quality in his "least of these" story found in the Gospel of Matthew:

> Then the king will say to those at his right hand, "Come, you that are blessed by my Father, inherit the kingdom prepared for you from the foundation of the world; for I was hungry and you gave me food, I was thirsty and you gave me something to drink, *I was a stranger and you welcomed me."* . . . Then the righteous will answer him, "Lord, when was it that we saw you hungry and gave you food, or thirsty and gave you something to drink? And when was it that we saw you *a stranger and welcomed you*?" . . . And the king will answer them, "Truly I tell you, just as you did it to one of the least of these *who are members of my family*, you did it to me."[2]

When we *love the stranger and welcome them*, we invite them in, we give them food and drink, we express the qualities of hospitality and engage with them on their own terms. When we do this, we are welcoming and loving members of God's family or, from the Christian perspective, we are welcoming members of Christ's family into our own families—and perhaps *Christ himself*. It becomes a mutually transforming process between those who were *othered* and those who are welcoming. Now those who are *loved* are also welcomed into the family.

---

1. 1 John 4:7–8; 16b–21.
2. Matt 25:34–40.

An interfaith practical theology of social change is based on the inherent worth of God's human family—that each one is deserving of love as well as *dignity*. They have the right to their own identity, and the ability to determine and define that identity according to their culture, religion, race, and nationality, and allow their experiences to expand their ideas of their own identity to broaden beyond customary ideas of those previously fixed categories of belonging. For example, when I was in my first year of seminary, in our spiritual formation class, another student, when listening to my background and my relationship with my *Hindu husband*, summed up my identity this way: "You cannot be a Christian because of your husband." His ideas of identity did not allow for an expanding notion of Christian identity to include those who love and are married to someone who is *religiously othered*. His response to my multicultural interfaith relationship stole my dignity. It took me many months to reclaim the dignity and worth of my marriage within my calling to *Christian ministry*. That was not the first nor the last occurrence where my legitimacy as a leader within the religious community was questioned because of who I loved. It is important for faith leaders and those who train them to remember that people within multicultural interfaith relationships have inherent worth and dignity and may have unique gifts to share with their communities.

A third principle of our emerging interfaith practical theology of social change is the importance of equity. For there to be an equal exchange of ideas and perspectives, we must be able to treat one another in equitable ways—recognizing that we are not equal and we have, instead, varying levels of privilege based on our class, religious community within our cultural context, our race, and whether our particular culture is one that is valued or one that is marginalized. Looking for ways to deconstruct power and inherent privilege in our communities allows us to respond in more equitable ways to people who may be marginalized within our societies. If we are among those who are privileged, we have a *duty* to stand up, speak up, and step in to allow for and *invite* the voices and cultures and religious practices of those who have been devalued into the conversation. Equity is a critical aspect of an interfaith practical theology of social change.

The fourth principle of our interfaith practical theology of social change is *duty*, or the responsibility of those who have experienced the benefit of growth and transformation from the multicultural interfaith encounters to *do something* to empower, support, and advocate for those who are *othered* based on their culture, class, caste, national origin, religion, or any other category that is used to exclude, harm, or otherwise commit violence upon a member of God's family. It is our *interfaith duty* to *be a social change agent* in our community. We have these gifts, and we are called to use them for good in the world.

A VIEW OF GOD

What might a view of God, Divinity, or the Sacred look like within an interfaith practical theology of social change? Since this theology believes in the power of love to transform hearts and minds, it follows that it would include a view of God that is inclusive, expansive, and changing. If experiences of love can change and transform former stereotypes about people who were formerly feared and oppressed, then our religious practices, traditions, and even our understandings of who God is in the world and God's view of *the other*, as expressed in our religious texts, can be reevaluated and reinterpreted based on this new information. Our faith traditions can grow, and, thus, so can our notions about God grow to be more expansive and inclusive in the process.

The couples, when asked about their understanding of God or the Sacred, offered a variety of responses. Our Catholic-Christian, Máire, has a sophisticated view of who Jesus is as a "kind, caring, and compassionate man," who invites us to work for justice. Her husband, A. S., a Hindu-Atheist, appreciates the role that faith plays in his wife's life and empowers her fully to raise their boys in the Christian tradition. He describes God "as a concept for explaining the world around us that is paralleled in nearly all societies." He has a strong ethic and believes in a "just world," and relates that to the themes he sees echoed in the faith of his wife of "a just God," and "a just society." Adam, who is Jewish, believes "G-d is a supernatural force that created humankind and the earth. G-d is an energy that enables us to have free will." His wife, Maria, who is a devout Catholic, has reevaluated her understanding of who Jesus is because of her many conversations with her Jewish husband. As has already been shared, "I believe in Jesus, that Jesus was the son of God and that he came down to earth. But I think that yes, there is a possibility that he wasn't the Messiah. I think that, I'm not sure if someone else doesn't believe it, they could be right." She is willing to have a healthy skepticism as part of her Christian faith.

An interfaith practical theology of social change suggests that by the dialogical process of questioning and considering, asserting and reevaluating individual values and beliefs, our multicultural interfaith couples will have a more thoughtful and considered ethic, or system of beliefs, and understanding of the Sacred divine force in their lives. These couples live inside of the gap—the fault lines of faith—where they must work to define and redefine who they are and what they believe. They can hold disparate views of Divinity together within the holy space of their family. They can live with paradox, appreciate dissent, and even come to enjoy the gift that arguments may bring. They are willing to not know the answer. They are willing to change their mind and allow others to do so as well. They learn to inhabit religious complexity. They do not expect simple answers, nor do they demand them. They enjoy the big questions. They are considerate, thoughtful, and measured in their approach to faith and practice. Ultimately, they are open to the conversation.

An interfaith practical theology of social change values a conversation about the Sacred and is willing to allow that conversation to change who and what the Sacred is. It is a theology that is alive, growing, and engaging. When we are willing to engage in the hard questions, including the ones about faith, God, the Sacred, service, justice, love, evil, corruption, suffering, and compassion, we are able to explore the depths of what it means to be human in our world. In the process, we discover a profound intimacy and come to value the complexity of human relationships. This is true love—a profound regard for one another. These are opportunities to explore the edges of the extraordinary and glimpse the realms of the holy. Ultimately, these kinds of arguments—this form of daily interfaith, intercultural dialogue—make us all better human beings and better equipped to lead lives of consequence and meaning.

Our faith traditions are often ill-equipped to deal with this level of religious complexity and consideration. Perhaps our clergy and faith leaders, seminaries and religious institutions of higher learning will need to engage in evaluative processes to see the blind spots with regards to welcoming or excluding of people who are *religiously othered* or considered *strangers* and *aliens in our land*. When our religious members bring one of these *othered people* into our place of worship and desire to marry them, are we welcoming them or does our religious tradition have policies and structures in place that cause further harm and exclusion? An interfaith practical theology of social change suggests that faith traditions themselves must also be willing to grow and change to meet the spiritual needs of God's people.

These are extraordinary people who are looking for deeper meaning and belonging for their family in the greater community.

MAKING ROOM FOR THE SPIRITUAL BUT NOT RELIGIOUS

An interfaith practical theology of social change makes room for people who are spiritual but not religious, who are atheist, agnostic, who belong to multiple religious traditions, or who have no religious affiliation at all. It values conversation, dialogue, perseverance, compassion, respect, and, most of all, honors the stories and journeys of those who have been marginalized. The importance of *deep listening* is a value of this theology because it is by our listening to one another's stories that we give the gifts of dignity and worth to those who have previously been excluded. We make room and space for their belonging. We give time for translation of different languages and cultural experiences. We value time together in shared cultural exchanges because we believe that these are *holy encounters*. This theology recognizes that, over time, tensions and conflicts may lessen, and appreciation, affinity, and even love may increase as mutual trust and stereotypes based on generations of trauma are healed within the multicultural interfaith human family. This theology believes that we are all created in the Divine's image, and that that image reflects the diversity and complexity of our world and its many varied cultures, traditions, races, nationalities, and religions.

WELCOME TENSION AND CONFLICT

This interfaith practical theology of social change expects that there will be tension and conflict. It is normal and promotes growth. It is authentic, it is real. We do not try to hide our differences, but are carefully and systematically willing to share and learn from one another, agreeing when we can, disagreeing when we must, finding common ground and allowing differences to remain, giving uniqueness and fresh perspectives to our experiences. This theology believes that faith is not just a private affair, but a public expression. It is an opportunity for public encounters and educational opportunities that can make growth and development possible within the community. This theology does not expect dogmatic adherence to traditions that may be based in colonial ideas of religious expression that have centered *privilege and whiteness* over many years. We welcome doubt, questions, and suspicion as healthy opportunities for engagement as long as they are done in the spirit of truth and do not intend to harm others.

Further, an emerging interfaith practical theology of social change anticipates mistakes and missteps. We believe in forgiveness and redemption. This theological methodology provides opportunities for evaluation and adaptation and is willing to identify when it does not serve the multicultural interfaith community. Finally, this theology builds on a pluralist liberation theology of religions and seeks justice, not only for people but also for the earth. This theology looks for leadership among those who would normally be excluded or prevented from being engaged in these kinds of faithful conversations because of their dual faiths or multiple rootedness and spiritual belonging. Their legitimacy is not questioned, but, rather, they are valued for their unique perspectives and nuanced understandings of the complexities found within our diverse worldviews.

19

Calling for Allies

UNTOUCHABILITY REVISITED

Nine years ago this past Christmas Eve, my *appa* died in India. We had just spent the previous eighteen months living together, arguing, attending medical visits side by side, shopping, walking, traveling, and even leading immersive cross-cultural interfaith experiences together at our local Hindu temple. We had just achieved a great accomplishment with him passing his US citizenship exam, and he had recently been sworn in as a citizen of this country. Now able to stay as long as he wished in the USA, his adopted country, he was also free to return to India to see his brother in time for his eightieth birthday, which is a significant religious occasion. After attending the function, he was fasting for a special *pooja*. Without me there to encourage him to eat a bit of fruit or nuts while fasting, he accidently fell and subsequently succumbed to his injuries. He and I had often clashed and conflicted on matters of gender equity and right practice of religious beliefs. We argued about the best ways to cook, clean, and work and play. We had long conversations about God, about American and Indian politics, and about his late wife, who I came to know as my *amma*. When they were both alive, she would take him aside to coach him while, simultaneously, my husband would take me aside and coach me, both of them saying "don't argue" with the other. Together we were similarly strong-willed, outspoken, confident, and passionate people, who were also very different. Yet, we loved our family deeply and with great devotion, which included an enduring love for one another. When he died, the tension between our two perspectives was no longer there. It was this multicultural interfaith tension, this persistent low level cross-cultural conflict that shaped and defined us and our understanding of the world. We were engaged in a daily interfaith dialogue that kept both of us involved in what we can now call an interfaith practical theology of social change. By means of mutual respect, love, dignity, equity, and a sense of duty to one another, our ideas about the *other* changed over time to such an extent that he *became the father to me that I never had.* There is something so valuable about having a conversation partner who is willing to challenge us to move outside of our comfortable positions and beliefs about God and the world.

Nineteen years prior to his death was the first time we met in India, in a little town called Perambur. Prior to my visit, they had little exposure to white women like me. The children ran through the streets of town pointing at me and crying out in Tamil, "pei, pei!" which means, "it's a ghost, a ghost!" While I was there, no matter how hard I tried to conform to the customs of this new family, a bit of my own culture and personality shown through. I was often louder than the other women, laughed too much, and touched people far more often than they touched even members of their own families. I expressed love through touch and especially through hugs. When departing from homes or returning from traveling I would hug my new aunts, my new mother-in-law, and even my new *paatti*, that is, Sriram's orthodox Hindu grandmother. She practiced ritual purity on a daily basis. After each of her daily baths she was ritually pure to perform her daily *poojas*. During this time, she would not touch nor be touched by anyone. Therefore, when I hugged her, no matter how much I desired to show love, her ritual purity would be disturbed. It is a little laughable now to talk about it, but the differences between our cultural and religious practices are reflected in this early encounter. Over time I learned about the Tamil concept of *muddhie*, which refers to being physically and ritualistically clean for conducting prayers, as well as for cooking food that is appropriate to serve to Brahmins. As I learned my role as the eldest son's wife and became more comfortable with the practices within the tradition, I knew when the times were more or less appropriate to hug my Indian family. When I reflected on that first visit and how much I did not know, I always felt a little embarrassed about what *I did wrong* during that time.

A year or so before *Appa* died, during the many months that we lived together, he shared with me a remarkable story. He asked if I remembered hugging his mother-in-law, *paatti*, during that first visit for our wedding in Perambur. Embarrassed, I answered, "yes, of course." It so happened that on that very first visit to India, five weeks after the wedding, when it came time to leave the country, *paatti* asked *Amma* in their native language of Tamil if I would give her a hug before I left. When I did, *paatti* stood there like a stiff board, arms by her side while I hugged her. I wondered if I had done the right thing even then. *Appa* continued, "Before you came to our family, *paatti* would not touch anyone, not the sons-in-law, not even her daughters. She did not show much physical affection. After you came into our family, she began to touch her daughters, kiss them, and even hugged them on occasion. She began hugging *Amma*, her own daughter." Having outlived her daughter by many years, *paatti* got to hug her daughter in the years just before *Amma* died. *Appa* continued, "All of this was because of *your love. You changed her for the better.*" Tears running down my cheeks, I was shocked and amazed. Until then I was very clear that their love for me *changed me and transformed my heart* in powerful and profound ways. It had never occurred to me that *I had changed them for the better too.* This is the power of multicultural interfaith love across all those boundaries of culture, race, nationality and religion. This is the story that I have been working to articulate in these pages—the extraordinary power of multicultural interfaith families to be positive social change agents within their communities.

What I have learned in the process is that multicultural interfaith families can be public theologians and prophetic voices emerging from the margins of our communities. In their daily living and loving, they are articulating an inclusive view of love, showing forth a greater purpose for their lives, redefining who God is for them, or demonstrating the ability to engage in *the sacred* or accessing the divine in new ways. They are envisioning a theology of religions that is more expansive than many of our traditional notions have previously suggested possible. Their methods of adapting and advocating, educating and engaging are ways of being faithful to their cultural and religious heritages. Over time they explore fundamental questions about identity and belonging. They observe ways in which the world is unjust and then work to *do something* to correct those injustices. In ways large and small, they seek to save and redeem themselves and their culture and institutions from the exclusionary practices that may have been obstacles in their own relationships. Some become spokespersons in their work and families—they become ambassadors of peace and justice, they stand up for the voiceless and the little guy. They call for a more loving and just world, and desire for reform and change in institutions that shut out *the other*. They become like Moses, like Ruth, and like Esther in another time—in our time. It is during this *New Prophetic Age*, in which we are living, that we must call forth *new leaders* who can navigate the cultural complexities of our day. We must call forth leaders who believe it is their duty to work for the equity and dignity of all persons. Perhaps one place we should be looking for this kind of nuanced leadership is within our multicultural interfaith families that live around the corner or in an urban center nearby.

A CALL FOR FAITH LEADERS TO BE ALLIES, NOT OBSTACLES

Ministers, rabbis, imams, priests, and other faith leaders would do well to consider the gifts that multicultural interfaith couples have to give to their communities. They can be catalysts for positive change in their communities when welcomed, blessed, empowered, and encouraged to use their skills of compassion, acceptance, and perseverance in the world. Multicultural interfaith couples could be the prophetic voices for healing and the bridge builders we need to shepherd us through the valleys of our cultural conflicts. Clergy are in a unique position to bless these young prophets and visionaries for peace. We can use our own prophetic imagination to call forth their voices and allow their gifts to help reshape our religious communities into ones that are more inclusive and more just. Some of our most creative and innovative programs often arise from the intersectionality of our experiences. Some specific things that faith leaders can do to support multicultural interfaith couples in the future include the table on the following page.

Faith leaders are representatives of institutional power. We have the power to bless or curse. Faith leaders can open doors or shut them and, in so doing, whether intending to or not, may either cause long-lasting harm or rather be examples of the inclusiveness and love of a compassionate and loving Creator. Standing on the principles of love, dignity, equity, and duty, faith leaders can advocate on behalf of multicultural interfaith couples to be welcomed, included, and belong *just as they are*, without feeling like they have to leave *the othered part* of their identity or relationship at home. In so doing, we may be catalyzing a movement for social change within our increasingly more culturally diverse and religiously complex communities. Who knows, in the process we may be welcoming and empowering the next intersectional leader who will become the bridge that crosses the fault lines between our global communities.

CALLING FOR ALLIES

Table 19.1 Faith Leaders as Allies of Interfaith Couples

Be an Ally, Not an Obstacle. Recognize that when a person approaches you with their young love story that crosses barriers of culture and religion, you can be a part of the healing and a support a new chapter in their faith journey.

Encourage. Encourage the families to participate in both religious traditions and to find communities of faith that will allow them to practice both faiths. Encourage them to learn to adapt and modify what they value from each tradition.

Bless. Bless the couples by finding ways to say yes when they come asking questions about interfaith marriages. Find examples in the community of successful interfaith relationships and invite them to speak during education or worship experiences.

Include Symbols from Multiple Traditions. When asked to perform religious rituals, such as weddings, naming ceremonies, baptisms, coming-of-age events, funerals or other rituals, invite symbols from the other partner's faith tradition to be incorporated. With the couple's blessing, invite other faith leaders to participate in the ceremony as well.

Suggest Two Ceremonies. Suggest that they take the time to conduct dual ceremonies in both traditions, if they desire to do so. Include the parents and families as much as possible, giving them the opportunity to learn and grow in their experience of both traditions, from the beginning of the couple's relationship.

Empower Leadership. Empower them to use their gifts for leadership in the community. Give them opportunities to lead, to speak, to educate, and to share their love story that crosses traditional cultural, racial, national, class, caste, or religious barriers.

Write Inclusively. When writing for the local media or submitting articles to be digitally published, write inclusively, recognizing the diversity of faiths living in the community.

Advocate. Anticipate the needs of the multicultural interfaith families already living in your community. Advocate for their inclusion and reach out to make them feel safe and welcome. Strategize with other faith leaders on how to lead by example with opportunities for interfaith encounters and engagement.

A WORD ON INTERFAITH LEADERSHIP

What value do you think multicultural interfaith couples contribute to their communities and what kind of leaders do we need today? I asked these two questions of each of my couples during the follow-up email after our ninety-minute interview sessions. At the time, our country had just witnessed the swearing in of President Joe Biden and Vice President Kamala Harris,[1] who

---

1. Kamala Harris is now running for president in the 2024 election. If elected she and her family will embody some of the multicultural interfaith values discussed herein. To learn more about Kamala Harris's intersectional life read, for instance: Mwaura, "Kamala Harris Talks."

is herself an intersectional leader raised in an interfaith Hindu/Christian home and married to a man who is Jewish. As a researcher looking at social change agency, I was curious what our multicultural interfaith couples believed our world needed now in the area of leadership. With regards to leadership, here are some of their responses: they were interested in the value of "good womanly" leaders; "leaders that see strength in diversity"; "we need true leaders who are fair and balanced . . . who are as concerned about the poor as they are with shareholders"; people "who stand up for democratic ideals and reinforce a separation of church and state"; "leadership holds the transformative power of examples of how life-giving diversity and difference can be"; interfaith leaders "demonstrate how differences can be bridged"; "we need men and women of fierce compassion—the ability to feel for the sufferings of others and then act fiercely out of compassion"; and "the United States now has leadership that not only respects and embraces diversity, but also reflects it." As we allow their words to echo in our hearts, words that are calling forth the kind of leadership we need today, we must also recognize that *they are the leaders they are calling forth.*

Multicultural interfaith couples already possess remarkable skills of fierce compassion and the ability to offer fair and balanced leadership considering the suffering and poor in their work. These couples see strength in diversity, they stand up for democratic ideals and demonstrate how differences can be bridged every day in their lives. These amazing people have the leadership qualities we are looking for to shape and shepherd us through our most difficult period in human history. They are beginning to hear the truth in that invitation to use their gifts to lead. Adam, in Costa Rica, serves on his inclusion and diversity task force at work and he taught me this valuable lesson when dealing with people who are different than ourselves, "Always assume good intent." When we can set our reactionary judgments to the side and assume, for the most part, that people do not intend harm, we may be able to listen more deeply to people who are different than us. Usha, married to Patrick, was nominated by her mayor to serve on their board of the Human Rights Commission. She felt she was now ready to step up and serve in this greater leadership role in her community and had the skills necessary to do so. These couples are ambassadors for good, agents of social change. Colleen, married to Shiva, our UU-Buddhist/Hindu couple reminds us, "We can be enriched by the *other*, and need not fear that something will be lost." Máire, married to A. S., our Catholic-Christian/Hindu-Atheist couple says it best,

> We serve as a bridge between two worlds. I have celebrated Sabbath dinner on a Friday evening and lit candles while praying in Hebrew. I have sat in front of a temple in my mother-in-law's temple room and listened to her sing in prayer. I have skipped a meal in solidarity with a friend who is fasting during Ramadan.

She is not alone in her assessment of the value of solidarity that multicultural couples can bring to our world. Interfaith couples can be ambassadors that cool the flames of conflict, bridge the fault lines between our civilizations, and raise the level of civil discourse in our communities that need good examples of how to live together, converse, diverge and converge, agree and disagree, and deepen our friendship with one another in the process.

WHERE DO WE GO FROM HERE?

This research used qualitative methods to explore the question: *Does sustained long-term interfaith dialogue within multicultural interfaith couples contribute to social change agency within communities?* Our interviewed couples suggest the answer is a resounding 'yes'. The survey results show that as the interfaith religious engagement increased among our multicultural interfaith couples, so did their social change agency in their communities. The correlation of religious engagement with social change agency goes beyond what theologians like Paul Knitter and practitioners like Eboo Patel and Susan Katz Miller assert, which is that interfaith religious engagement, or interfaith dialogue, enriches the participants. This research suggests that not only does it enrich the participants, but it enriches their communities as well. By developing leadership skills such as persevering during conflict, developing compassionate responses, and navigating cultural and religious difference, they become social change agents and use their abilities to advocate, educate, host, negotiate, and lead within their communities. Further, we see examples of this kind of leadership within our scriptural texts. By applying an interfaith theological method of exegetical analysis to traditional scriptural stories, biblical examples of multicultural interfaith leaders like Moses, Ruth, and Esther become evident. Finally, an interfaith practical theology of social change can be used by faith leaders, theologians, and interfaith practitioners as a way to further this emerging field of interfaith studies and broaden our capacity to impart wisdom, cultivate nuanced leadership, and contribute to the growth and sustainability of our increasingly diverse global community. Using the four principles of love, dignity, equity, and duty to guide our actions, I believe this interfaith practical theology of social change can make a profound difference by transforming our diverse global communities into more peaceful, kinder, and more equitable places for all of our human family.

AREAS FOR FURTHER STUDY

My particular area of interest in multicultural interfaith couples includes people who form relationships with individuals from countries in South Asia, including India, though uncommon relationships across differences are generally of interest to me. Future areas of study would include exploring this interfaith practical theology of social change with queer couples who cross barriers of race, culture, religion, gender, and sexuality. It would be helpful to academics and researchers like myself to promote the inclusion of multiple religious belonging/spiritual fluidity in larger surveys, such as those that come from the Pew Research Center and other bodies that assess marriage trends around the world. Multicultural interfaith couples are unique and lack the kind of community support and relationships that could empower them to fully develop their abilities to realize their potential for leadership. Interfaith community networks where couples who face similar challenges can find each other is of great need, particularly with those who marry people from traditional cultures similar to those found in South Asia. Additionally, exploring the leadership skills identified in this research, and their application to people who are effective at brokering solutions in highly complex and nuanced situations across culture and religion, would be beneficial. Are our most effective social change agents and leaders able to see and perceive their most complex leadership challenges from an intersectional understanding across distinct cultural, racial, and religious perspectives? In other words, does a multicultural interfaith worldview give rise to effective leadership at the highest levels of government, business, education, and religious encounters? My immediate hope is this work will empower multicultural interfaith couples to find each other and encourage community leaders to welcome them as the gifts they are to the world.

20

Advice for Couples and Families

WHAT ADVICE DO I give to couples at the beginning of their multicultural interfaith journey together regarding their parents, who may disapprove of their chosen partner? Remember that most parents want their adult children to live their best life, to love and be loved. In their fear and concern for you, what they say may sound hurtful. It may be coming from a place to protect their culture and provide for a good life for their family, including you. Much of what is taught in conservative religious traditions around the world suggest that the only way that you can live a good and holy life is to have a family life that is consistent with those traditional beliefs. They may believe that the house should not be divided; if the house is divided, then there will be unhappiness in the family. They may think your marriage will not last. People said this to me and my husband. We have enjoyed our multicultural interfaith life for over twenty-seven years. There is this idea that if you cannot maintain the religious traditions and the purity of that religious expression because you married outside the community, there will be loss of culture and faith that will ultimately occur. But what is almost never considered in the beginning of newly forming multicultural interfaith relationships, is that when two people come together from very different backgrounds, they can enhance one other's religious experiences. They can help one another be more faithful. They can learn from one another and share in conversations back and forth that help to strengthen those cultural beliefs and find new ways of adapting. What we find over time is that when couples persist in being authentic to themselves, to their own version of their faith and practice of culture, when they consistently share that with their families and communities, their communities adapt, learn, grow, and expand their own ideas about what is possible. Do not give up on your elders. Keep sharing. Over time, research suggests they will grow with you.

What advice might I give to parents of adult children marrying outside the religious and cultural community? You are not alone in your worries and concerns. Many parents have grown to love and cherish their expanding multicultural interfaith family. Over time they even find great joy in it! Do not shy away from talking about the differences between these two different faith traditions and cultures. Talk with your adult child about your values. Spend time with their partner and ask questions about what they love about your child. You may find they actually love their cultural expressions and religious identity. Adopt a habit of being curious, versus being critical. You can accomplish this by letting go of the worry about the future and begin to ask questions intended to help you learn about your child's chosen partner. Take the time to work through the tensions and the conflicts out of love. Bring compassion to their young relationship. You were young once also! You have great wisdom to share. Encourage your child to have the religious and cultural expressions of both families, both cultures, and both languages present in the wedding ceremony, or, if possible, host two ceremonies. It will allow the new couple and their two families to begin to deal with real differences and find ways to adapt. The tendency in the beginning will be to see the similarities between your two cultures and to avoid the conflicts of where there are important differences. That will only get you so far. How you can help build a long and happy married life for your child is by carefully working through those tensions and conflicts and being able to talk about them compassionately and directly. One way to do that is to strive to honor both cultures and faith traditions. Encourage the new couple to reinterpret your traditions, to adapt them to fit with who they are now. Religions tend to be resilient over time and the essence of what is true and meaningful is retained with every generation.

To the amazing multicultural interfaith couples reading this, every life stage is an opportunity for you to be a social change agent in the world. You are the nuanced leader we need in this complex world. Remember to honor one another's culture and faith traditions each year you are married. When you go through life stages, when you have children (if you have children), when you experience losses, move into new homes, celebrate new jobs or graduations, and even funerals, each of these life events are opportunities for you to share and express your own faith and culture. Be honest with your partner about where there are differences and where you believe or do not believe in similar ways to your family, or to your partner. Notice the injustices around you. Advocate for people in your community who are not being treated fairly. You have learned to do this with your partner, whom you love dearly; you can do this for others too. You have specialized gifts. Use them for good. Keep expressing and reimagining your beliefs in a way that includes people from other religious traditions and people who do not believe as you do. Thank you for your courage and for living a life that brings more love and justice into this world.

Appendix A: Photos of Multicultural Interfaith Couples

1: Engagement photo of Kamalpreet and Kamran, Sikh/Muslim couple in Washington State

APPENDIX A: PHOTOS OF MULTICULTURAL INTERFAITH COUPLES

2: Wedding of Colleen and Shiva, and 3: Hindu wedding reenactment in honor of Shiva's 50th birthday. UU-Buddhist/Hindu couple in Texas

 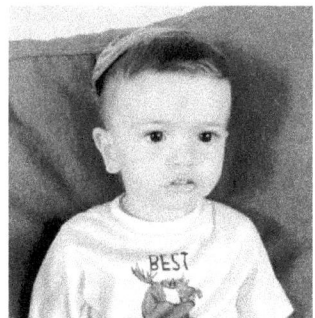

4: Wedding and 5: Son of Maria and Adam with "kippa," Catholic/Jewish couple in Costa Rica

Appendix A: Photos of Multicultural Interfaith Couples

6: Wedding and 7: Christening of A. S. and
Máire's son, Hindu-Atheist/Catholic-Christian couple

8: Cathy and Paul, Buddhist/Buddhist-Catholic couple
in South Korean Zen Monastery 2010

APPENDIX A: PHOTOS OF MULTICULTURAL INTERFAITH COUPLES

9 and 10: Prayer Space of Arundhati and Sanjaya,
Christian/Hindu-Atheist Couple in India

11: Blended family of Usha and Patrick,
UU-Hindu/Catholic-Christian Couple in the Midwest

Appendix B: Qualitative Interview Summary Topics

Relationship Formation

1. Tell me a little about how you met.
2. Were there people in your respective lives that were surprised or concerned about the two of you coming together as couple?

Perceived Experiences with Cultural Tension and Conflict

3. What are the biggest perceived differences between people of your two cultures/religions marrying? What are some common misconceptions?
4. When you think about your time together, what has been the source of the greatest joys? the greatest tensions?

Leadership and Social Change Advocacy

5. In what ways do you think your couple has impacted your family, workplaces, or community around you?
6. Can you tell me about someone in your life who would have disapproved strongly of your relationship, or who may have had a change of heart? What happened?
7. Can you think of a time when you have stood up for the rights of another person? Someone whom you thought was being treated unfairly?

APPENDIX B: QUALITATIVE INTERVIEW SUMMARY TOPICS

Theology and Suffering

8. How has your view of God/spirituality changed over the course of your relationship?
9. Have you been a witness to suffering or conflict that you perceived as being based on race, culture, caste, or religion?
10. What cultural conflicts do you notice going on in our world? How do(es) your values/faith/spirituality shape your worldview?

Appendix C: Survey Questions on Interfaith Religious Engagement

1. Did your couple have a religious wedding/marriage ceremony? With answers of "Yes"; "No"; and "Yes, we had two religious ceremonies—one for each of our traditions."
2. Do you participate in your partner's religious functions/holidays/services?
3. Does your partner participate in your partner's religious functions/holidays/services?

The following four questions invite a response of "daily; weekly; monthly; a few times a year; during high holy days; or only when there is a special event like a funeral, wedding, or birth."

4. How often do you and your partner talk about faith/spirituality/God/religion?
5. How often do you and your partner attend religious services/functions/events together?
6. How often do you and/or your partner perform a religious ritual in your home?
7. How often do you engage a spiritual practice such as prayer/meditation/chanting or reading of a sacred text?
8. How often does your partner engage a spiritual practice such as prayer/meditation/chanting or reading of a sacred text?

Appendix D: Questions on Tension and Conflict

1. Early on in your relationship, how was your couple perceived by your family?

    Measured on a 7-point positivity/negativity scale.

2. Early on in your relationship, how was your couple perceived by your spouse's family?

    With a 7-point positivity/negativity scale.

3. My family would have preferred that my partner was of their same religious tradition.

    a. yes, definitely

    b. perhaps, it would have been easier

    c. no, not at all.

4. My partner's family would have preferred that I was of their same religious tradition.

    a. yes, definitely

    b. perhaps, it would have been easier

    c. no, not at all.

Appendix D: Questions on Tension and Conflict

5. My family, at some point, asked if my partner would adopt/convert to their religious tradition.

   a. They asked my partner directly to convert or change religious traditions.

   b. They mentioned to me that it would be better if my partner converted or changed their religious traditions.

   c. They did not ask them to adopt or convert.

6. My partner's family, at some point, asked if I would adopt/convert to their religious tradition.

   a. They asked me directly to convert or change religious traditions.

   b. They mentioned to my partner that it would be better if I converted or changed their religious traditions.

   c. They did not ask me to adopt or convert.

7. Has your couple experienced instances of prejudice that you perceive to be related to your religious affiliation, racial background, caste, or cultural or ethnic identity?

   With answers on a sliding scale of 1–100, with 1 being "We have rarely experienced instances of prejudice based on our religious, racial, or ethnic identities"; 50 being "We have experienced some instances"; and 100 being "We often experience instances of prejudice based on our religious, racial, or ethnic identities."

8. Describe an example of prejudice or discrimination you or your partner has experienced.

Appendix E: Questions on Social Change Agency

1. Would you say that your family's views of your relationship have changed over time?
2. Would you say that your partner's family's views of your relationship have changed over time?

   These two questions had the following as possible answers:

   a. Yes, they have grown to accept and appreciate our relationship over time.
   b. Yes, they have changed their view of our relationship—they view our relationship more negatively now than before.
   c. Somewhat. Some members are accepting and supportive, but others remain reluctant to accept our relationship even after some time has passed.
   d. No, their view of our relationship has remained unchanged from the beginning—they have always been supportive.
   e. No, their view of our relationship has remained unchanged from the beginning—they continue to be unsupportive.
   f. We have little to no contact with members of that side of the family.

3. Have you or your partner sought an exception to a rule or policy, that you thought was unfair toward your family, related to your culture, race, caste, class, or religious practices? Perhaps with a religious institution, a school, within your own families, or workplace?

Appendix E: Questions on Social Change Agency

4. Have you or your partner supported a person outside of your immediate family to seek an exception to a rule or policy, that they perceived was unfair, based on culture, race, caste, class, or religious practices? Perhaps with a religious institution, a school, within their own families, or workplace?

For the following five questions, open text boxes were provided for free-written answers.

5. What kind of volunteer activities have you or your partner engaged in over the course of your relationship?
6. Have you or your partner been involved in any social justice activities/causes or social change movements? These could be programs that focus on empowerment, equal access, policy change, and/or economic development as part of a national movement, or at the local level (i.e., a school referendum, running for local government position, etc.).
7. Are either you or your partner a leader of a social justice movement/cause, or advocacy program?
8. Have you or your partner supported or advocated for the rights of another person whom you perceived was being treated unfairly by the system based on their race, caste, class, or religious affiliation?
9. If yes, did you feel that your interfaith relationship helped you to better understand the situation? Please briefly explain.
10. Would you say that you have grown in your faith over the life of your partnership? On a sliding scale of 1–100, with 1 being "Becoming less and less important"; 50 being "Remained the same"; and 100 being "Becoming more and more important."
11. Would you say that your partner has grown in their faith over the life of your partnership? On a sliding scale of 1–100, with 1 being "Becoming less and less important"; 50 being "Remained the same"; and 100 being "Becoming more and more important."

Appendix F: Eight Couples Selected for In-Depth Interviews

Arundhati and Sanjaya
Christian/Hindu-Atheist
An Indian Protestant Christian married to an Indian Lingayat Hindu-Atheist.
They reside in South India and have been married for thirty years.
Recorded August 6, 2020, over Zoom and transcribed using Descript.

Colleen and Shiva
UU-Buddhist/Hindu
An American UU-Buddhist (raised Catholic) married to an Indian Tamil Iyer Brahmin.
They reside in Texas with their teenaged son and have been married for twenty years.
Recorded October 4, 2020, over Zoom and transcribed using Descript.

Máire and A. S.
Catholic-Episcopalian/Hindu-Atheist
An American Catholic Episcopalian married to an Indian Hindu-Atheist.
They reside in Ohio with young boys and have been married for twelve years.
Recorded October 12, 2020, over Zoom and transcribed using Descript.

Cathy and Paul
Buddhist/Buddhist-Catholic
An American Buddhist (formerly Catholic) married to an American Buddhist-Catholic.
They reside in Wisconsin and have been married for forty years.
Recorded October 26, 2020, over Zoom and transcribed using Descript.

Appendix F: Eight Couples Selected for In-Depth Interviews

Usha and Patrick
UU-Hindu/Catholic-Christian
An Indian UU Bada Paliwal Brahmin Hindu married to an American Catholic Christian.
They reside in the Midwest with two young boys and have been married for twenty years.
Recorded October 30, 2020, over Zoom and transcribed using Descript.

Kamalpreet and Kamran
Sikh/Muslim
An Americanized Indian Punjabi Sikh engaged to a Pakistani-heritage American Muslim.
They reside in Washington and are newly engaged, but have been together for eight years.
Recorded November 4, 2020, over Zoom and transcribed using Descript.

Maria and Adam
Catholic/Jewish
A Spanish-speaking Costa Rican Catholic married to an English-speaking American Jew.
They reside in Costa Rica with their eighteen-month-old son and have been married for two years.
Recorded November 9, 2020, on Zoom in Spanish and English. Translated and transcribed using Descript.

Geetha and Peter
Hindu/Evangelical Christian
An English- and Tamil-speaking Indian American Hindu married to a English and Mandarin speaking Taiwanese Evangelical Christian whose father is a minister. They are newly married and reside in Georgia.
Recorded on February 26, 2024, on Zoom and transcribed by this author.

Glossary of Terms

ABCD — This acronym stands for American Born Confused Desi. This is a term often used by Indian citizens who study in the United States to refer to people of Indian origin, who are born to Indian parents, in the United States. It points to the cultural tension between the cultures of India and America that can result in a period of questioning one's identity.

Agni — A Sanskrit name for the invocation of the holy god of fire. A fire is established by the priest and is required as the holy witness of any sacred act, such as weddings, funerals, coming of age rituals, and other poojas. *Agni* is one of the holy elements. The others are *Vaayu,* the holy wind, *Bhoomi,* the holy earth, *Akash,* the holy sky, and *Teertham,* the holy water. *Surya,* in reference to the sacred sun, is also important as it is the source of all life.

Ayodhya — Both a physical location in North India and a spiritual location associated with the birthplace of Lord Ram. This is the city which contains the site of the Babri Masjid Incident, where an ancient mosque from the Mughal period was destroyed by Hindu nationals.

Bada Paliwal An upper caste Brahmin community from Rajasthan in North India.

Brahmin — Considered to be the "highest caste" in India. Brahmins have historically, in India, held the most privilege and come under considerable criticism for their treatment of other castes, especially the group that was referred to as "untouchable." Untouchability was outlawed in 1950 in the Indian Constitution.[1]

---

1. Vikaspedia Indian Online Encyclopedia, "Caste System in India."

Glossary of Terms

co-sister   A daughter-in-law's relationship to another daughter-in-law in the family who is married to the brother of her husband. It is a term that originated in joint families.

Dalit   A term referring to those who were previously considered "untouchable" within the Hindu caste system. The term dalit means "broken or downtrodden."[2]

Desi   Anyone from India. 'Des' is the Hindi word for 'homeland' and an affectionate term for India. So, a *desi* is anyone who is from India.

Diwali   A Hindi term referring to the Indian holiday occurring in the month of October or November, celebrated by Hindus and other Indian religious traditions, commemorating the triumph of good over evil. It is also referred to as the "Festival of Lights," in part, because of the lighting of little oil lamps, in Hindi, called *diyas*, or, in Tamil, called *deepas*. The holiday is also referred to as *Deepavali* in South India.

diya   A little oil lamp often traditionally made from earthen clay, filled with oil and a wick, and then lit during the festival of *Diwali*, a.k.a. *Deepavali*. They are often decoratively painted and paired with tea light candles or electric tea lights, instead of using oil and a wick. They are lined up all around the house and light after dusk. Also known as a *deepa*.

dosai   A thin South Indian pancake, which is made from fermented rice and white lentils called urid dal. It is traditionally served with coconut chutney, potato subgee, and a spicy lentil soup called sambar.

gurudwara   A Sikh place of worship, similar to a temple or a mosque in that this is where people of the faith community gather, worship, sing, and, especially, join in *lungar* (shared community meals where everyone is welcome, no matter their background or faith tradition).

joint family   A multigenerational family where the elder parents, often but not always the parents of the husband, live with the family. There may be multiple young families, usually brothers of each other with their wives living together with their parents

---

2. Kim, "India," 47.

Glossary of Terms

and children. The children who are cousins grow up together as sisters and brothers.

Iyengar — One of two South Indian Tamil Brahmin communities originating in the state of Tamil Nadu. They speak the language Tamil. They are *Vaishnavite*, that is, they worship the God Vishnu, the Sustainer of the Universe.

Iyer — One of two South Indian Tamil Brahmin communities originating in the state of Tamil Nadu. They speak the language Tamil. They are *Shaivite*, that is, they worship the God Shiva, the Destroyer or Dissolver of the Universe.

kara — A traditional Sikh piece of jewelry, which is a silver bangle, worn by both men and women within the religious tradition. It is one of the Five K's that are part of adherent Sikh identity.

kalish — A traditional water vessel used during Hindu prayer ceremonies made of silver, copper, steel, or plastic. They are wider at the bottom and have a narrow neck that opens again with a wide rim. Coming in various sizes, they are used to store water, to hold whole coconuts during poojas, and for bathing. Those used for poojas are usually made of silver and are engraved with ornate carvings.

Laxmi — The Hindu Goddess of abundance, wealth and prosperity. She is often depicted either seated or standing within a lotus blossom, a spiritual symbol of resilience and beauty.

Lingayat — A term referring to a new orthodox community of Hindus who reject traditional understanding of Brahminism. They were established in the twelfth century as an anti-Brahmin sect within the Shaivite tradition—those who worship Shiva and the symbolic Shivalingam. They allow for conversion.

masjid — An Arabic word for mosque, or Islamic place of worship.

mohel — A Jewish practitioner of circumcision on baby boys, traditionally conducted on the eighth day, in the ceremony called a *bris*.

muddhie — A Tamil word referring to a very strict form of bathing and washing cloths, which includes hanging them where no one can touch them. Once the clothes are worn, they must remain untouched by anyone who is *not muddhie* or by someone who

Glossary of Terms

	is not similarly ritualistically clean. Once a person bathes and puts on *muddhie* clothes, they are ready to perform *poojas* and are able to cook for special holidays, as well as feed Brahmin community members.
Pandavas	A term referring to the five brothers who are the main heroic characters of the Hindu epic *Mahabharatha*, one of the sacred stories of Hinduism. It is a religious tale of good versus evil, an exploration of just wars and ethical behavior in the face of envy, greed, and temptation.
Parigharam	This is a Tamil word referring to the ability to remove spiritual obstacles, or evil forces at work in one's life by performing special prayers, religious ceremonies, visiting certain holy sites, and may include wearing certain pieces of jewelry for a fixed period of time.
paatti	A Tamil word that simply means "grandmother."
pooja	A Hindi word that means "prayer ritual," often conducted within the home.
rokha	A Hindi word meaning "stop," which refers to an Indian custom of arranging marriages when the two families agree to stop receiving profiles for potential marriage partners for their adult child.
sambar	A South Indian vegetarian lentil stew made with toor dal, a yellow lentil this is used frequently in South Indian dishes.
seva	Acts of holy service from the Indian Hindu religious context.
Shivalingam	A symbol of the Shiva, the Hindu God of destruction or dissolution that is represented by the combination of a phallus inside of a vulva base representing the divine combination of the masculine and feminine qualities of God.
tallit	A Jewish shawl that has fringes with knots that represent the commandments from the Torah. A new *bar* or *bat mitzvah* will often receive one as a gift at the time of the rite of passage into their adult religious role.
Tamil	A South Indian language spoken by people who originated from the state of Tamil Nadu. It is a very ancient language; some say older than Sanskrit, which is the language in which

Glossary of Terms

many of the religious texts are written. Words can be found in both traditions that show these two ancient languages influenced each other.

tatha   A Tamil word that simply means "grandfather."

tzedakah   A Hebrew word within the Jewish tradition which refers to sacred service and, according to Jonathan Sacks, "distributive justice."[3]

---

3. Sacks, *Dignity of Difference*, 113.

Bibliography

Bidwell, Duane R. *When One Religion Isn't Enough: The Lives of Spiritually Fluid People.* Boston: Beacon, 2019.

Brazal, Agnes M. "Ecological Cultural Struggles of Indigenous Peoples: Toward Sustainability as Flourishing." In *A Theology of Southeast Asia: Liberation-Postcolonial Ethics in the Philippines*, 89–115. Maryknoll, NY: Orbis, 2019.

Brueggemann, Walter. *The Prophetic Imagination: 40th Anniversary Edition.* Minneapolis: Fortress, 2018.

Cone, James H. *Black Theology and Black Power.* Maryknoll, NY: Orbis, 1997.

Crawford, Sidnie Ann White. "Esther." In *Women's Bible Commentary: Expanded Edition*, edited by Carol Ann Newsom and Sharon H. Ringe, 131–37. Louisville: Westminster John Knox, 1998.

Douglas, Kelly Brown. *The Black Christ.* Maryknoll, NY: Orbis, 1994.

Du Bois, W. E. B. "Strivings of the Negro People." *Atlantic*, Aug. 1897. https://www.theatlantic.com/magazine/archive/1897/08/strivings-of-the-negro-people/305446/.

Eck, Diana L. *Encountering God: A Spiritual Journey from Bozeman to Banaras.* Boston: Beacon, 2003.

"The 18th and 19th Centuries." In "Sikhism," in "History and Doctrine." *Encyclopædia Britannica.* Accessed Aug. 11, 2024. https://www.britannica.com/topic/Sikhism/The-18th-and-19th-centuries.

Fausset, Richard, et al. "Democrats Win Both Georgia Races to Gain Control of Senate." *New York Times*, Jan. 6, 2021. https://www.nytimes.com/2021/01/06/us/politics/warnock-loeffler-ossoff-perdue-georgia-senate.html.

Fears, Darryl. "One Million Species Face Extinction, U.N. Report Says. And Humans Will Suffer as a Result." *Washington Post*, May 6, 2019. https://www.washingtonpost.com/climate-environment/2019/05/06/one-million-species-face-extinction-un-panel-says-humans-will-suffer-result/?utm_term=.cd55f38c0248.

Fernandez, Eleazar S. *Burning Center, Porous Borders.* Eugene, OR: Wipf & Stock, 2011. Kindle.

Frayer, Lauren. "A New Law in India Is Making It Harder for Interfaith Couples to Get Married." *NPR*, Sept. 14, 2021. https://www.npr.org/2021/09/14/1037096376/a-new-law-in-india-is-making-it-harder-for-interfaith-couples-to-get-married#:~:text=Live%20Sessions-,A%20New%20Law%20In%20India%20Is%20Making%20It%20Harder%20For,is%20to%20halt%20forced%20conversions.

Gafney, Wilda C. *Daughters of Miriam: Women Prophets in Ancient Israel.* Minneapolis: Fortress, 2008.

Bibliography

———. *Womanist Midrash: A Reintroduction to the Women of the Torah and the Throne.* Louisville: Westminster John Knox, 2017.
Grey, Mary. "Gandhi, Ecofeminism and the Elusiveness of Truth." In *Waging Peace Building a World in Which Life Matters: Festschrift to Honour Gabriele Dietrich,* edited by Gabriele Dietrich, et al., 115–34. Delhi: IWIT/ISPCK, 2004.
Hạnh, Nhất. *Living Buddha, Living Christ.* New York: Riverhead, 2007.
Huntington, Samuel Phillips, and Zbigniew Brzezinski. *The Clash of Civilizations and the Remaking of World Order.* New York: Simon & Schuster, 2011.
Jacob, Sharon. "Neither Here nor There! A Hermeneutics of Shuttling: Reflections of an Indian Postcolonial Feminist Biblical Critic." In *Asian and Asian American Women in Theology and Religion,* edited by Pui-lan Kwok, 123–36. Cham, Switzerland: Palgrave Macmillan, 2020. https://doi.org/10.1007/978-3-030-36818-0_9.
Johnson, Neil. "Hundreds Protest Trump, Ryan in Janesville." *GazetteXtra,* Feb. 4, 2017. https://www.gazettextra.com/archives/hundreds-protest-trump-ryan-in-janesville/article_fff5c67b-0943-5519-bcc4-2fcc6ff36aee.html.
Kim, Grace Ji-Sun, and Susan M. Shaw. *Intersectional Theology: An Introductory Guide.* Minneapolis: Fortress, 2018. Kindle.
Kim, Kirsteen. "India." In *An Introduction to Third World Theologies,* edited by John Parratt, 44–73. Cambridge, UK: Cambridge University Press, 2005.
King, Martin Luther, Jr. *The Radical King.* Edited by Cornel West. Boston: Beacon, 2016.
Klobuchar, Amy. "Senator Klobuchar Delivers Remarks at Inauguration of President Joseph R. Biden and Vice President Kamala Harris." U.S. Senator Amy Klobuchar, Jan. 20, 2021. https://www.klobuchar.senate.gov/public/index.cfm/2021/1/senator-klobuchar-delivers-remarks-at-inauguration-of-president-joseph-r-biden-and-vice-president-kamala-harris.
Knitter, Paul F. *One Earth, Many Religions: Multifaith Dialogue and Global Responsibility.* New York: Orbis, 1995.
———. *Introducing Theologies of Religions.* Maryknoll, NY: Orbis, 2002.
———. "Toward a Liberation Theology of Religions." In *The Myth of Christian Uniqueness,* edited by John Hick and Paul F. Knitter, 178–200. London: SCM, 2008.
———. *Without Buddha I Could Not Be a Christian.* New York: Oneworld, 2009.
Krishnan, Murali. "Why Interfaith Marriage in India Is Getting Dangerous." *DW,* Jan. 11, 2023. https://www.dw.com/en/why-interfaith-marriage-in-india-is-getting-dangerous/a-64350804.
Levine, Amy-Jill. "Ruth." In *Women's Bible Commentary: Expanded Edition,* edited by Carol Ann Newsom and Sharon H. Ringe, 84–90. Louisville: Westminster John Knox, 1998.
"Lingayats." In "Worldmark Encyclopedia of Cultures and Daily Life." Encyclopedia.com. Accessed Aug. 30, 2024. https://www.encyclopedia.com/humanities/encyclopedias-almanacs-transcripts-and-maps/lingayats.
Lucero, Cecilia. "The Letter to My Freshman Self (That Will Never Appear in a Notre Dame Publication)." *Show Some Skin: Drop the Wall,* Feb. 20–23, 2019. Posted Mar. 16, 2019. YouTube. https://www.youtube.com/watch?v=Xdi72ShyEE4&list=PLWEkyQAOWQgbt4-_gkUAxy5gdbG5OemsI&index=38.
Miller, Susan Katz. *Being Both: Embracing Two Religions in One Interfaith Family.* Boston: Beacon, 2014.

Bibliography

Modi, Radha, et al. "Communities on Fire: Confronting Hate Violence and Xenophobic Political Rhetoric." SAALT, 2018. Accessed Feb. 9, 2021. https://saalt.org/wp-content/uploads/2018/01/Communities-on-Fire.pdf.

Mwaura, Maina. "Kamala Harris Talks about Her Own Faith and How It Might Influence a Biden-Harris White House." *Religion News Service*, November 7, 2020. https://religionnews.com/2020/10/28/kamala-harris-talks-about-her-own-faith-and-how-it-might-influence-a-biden-harris-white-house/.

Nair, Aishwarya. "Ayodhya or 'Vatican City for Hindus'? How Is the UP Government Planning to Make the City a Global Religious Centre?" *Youth Media Channel* (blog). *ED Times*, Jan. 25, 2021. https://edtimes.in/ayodhya-or-vatican-city-for-hindus-how-is-the-up-government-planning-to-make-the-city-a-global-religious-centre/.

The New Oxford Annotated Bible. 3rd rev. ed. New York: Oxford University Press, 2001.

Newcom, Steve. *Sevenfold: Dimensions and Dynamics of Social Transformation*. Minneapolis: Kaleo Center, 2020.

Newman, Andy. "Highlights: Reaction to Trump's Travel Ban." *New York Times*, Jan. 29, 2017. https://www.nytimes.com/2017/01/29/nyregion/trump-travel-ban-protests-briefing.html.

Panikkar, Raimundo. "The Jordan, the Tiber, and the Ganges." In *The Myth of Christian Uniqueness: Toward a Pluralistic Theology of Religions*, edited by John Hick and Paul F. Knitter, 89–116. Eugene, OR: Wipf & Stock, 2005.

Patel, Eboo. *Interfaith Leadership: A Primer*. Boston: Beacon, 2016.

Pew Research Center. "One-in-Five U.S. Adults Were Raised in Interfaith Homes." Oct. 26, 2016. https://www.pewresearch.org/religion/2016/10/26/one-in-five-u-s-adults-were-raised-in-interfaith-homes/.

———. "Chapter 2: Religious Switching and Intermarriage." In *America's Changing Religious Landscape*, May 12, 2015. https://www.pewforum.org/2015/05/12/chapter-2-religious-switching-and-intermarriage/.

———. "'Nones' on the Rise." Oct. 9, 2012. https://www.pewforum.org/2012/10/09/nones-on-the-rise/.

Pieris, Aloysius. *An Asian Theology of Liberation*. Edinburgh: T&T Clark, 1988.

Pillalamarri, Akhilesh. "India's Anti-Sikh Riots, 30 Years On." *Diplomat*, Oct. 31, 2014. https://thediplomat.com/2014/10/indias-anti-sikh-riots-30-years-on/.

Press Trust of India. "Babri Masjid Demolition Case: A Timeline of Events from 1528 to 2020." *Business Standard*, Sept. 30, 2020. https://www.business-standard.com/article/current-affairs/babri-masjid-demolition-case-a-timeline-of-events-from-1528-to-2020-120093000616_1.html.

Population of the World. "Population of India." https://www.livepopulation.com/country/india.html.

Rosenberg, Eli. "Protest Grows 'Out of Nowhere' at Kennedy Airport after Iraqis Are Detained." *New York Times*, Jan. 29, 2017. https://www.nytimes.com/2017/01/28/nyregion/jfk-protests-trump-refugee-ban.html.

Rowell, James L. "Sikhism." In *Making Sense of the Sacred: The Meaning of World Religions*, 161–80. Minneapolis: 1517 Media, 2021. https://doi.org/10.2307/j.ctv17vf47z.13.

Ruether, Rosemary Radford. "Feminism and Jewish-Christian Dialogue." In *The Myth of Christian Uniqueness: Toward a Pluralistic Theology of Religions*, edited by John Hick and Paul F. Knitter, 137–48. Eugene, OR: Wipf & Stock, 2005.

Sacks, Jonathan. *The Dignity of Difference: How to Avoid the Clash of Civilizations*. London: Bloomsbury, 2003.

Bibliography

Sikhism Guide. "Five Sikh Symbols." Accessed Aug. 30, 2024. https://sikhismguide.neocities.org/fiveks.

Slessarev-Jamir, Helene. *Prophetic Activism: Progressive Religious Justice Movements in Contemporary America*. New York: New York University Press, 2011.

Steinmetz, Katy. "She Coined the Term 'Intersectionality' over 30 Years Ago. Here's What It Means to Her Today." *Time*, Feb. 20, 2020. https://time.com/5786710/kimberle-crenshaw-intersectionality/.

Suchocki, Marjorie Hewitt. *Divinity and Diversity: A Christian Affirmation of Religious Pluralism*. Nashville: Abingdon, 2003.

Thurman, Howard. *Jesus and the Disinherited*. Boston: Beacon, 1996.

Trump, Donald. "Protecting the Nation from Foreign Terrorist Entry into the United States." Exec. Order 13,769. Fed. Reg. Feb. 2, 2017. https://www.federalregister.gov/documents/2017/02/01/2017-02281/protecting-the-nation-from-foreign-terrorist-entry-into-the-united-states.

Tully, Mark. "How the Babri Mosque Destruction Shaped India." *BBC*, Dec. 5, 2017. https://www.bbc.com/news/world-asia-india-42219773.

Vikaspedia Indian Online Encyclopedia. "Caste System in India." English. Accessed Feb. 19, 2021. https://vikaspedia.in/social-welfare/social-awareness/caste-system-in-india#:~:text=Caste%20system%20in%20India%20%E2%80%94%20Vikaspedia.

Wheeler, Demian. *Religion within the Limits of History Alone. Pragmatic Historicism and the Future of Theology*. Albany: State University of New York Press, 2020.

Wikipedia. "Costa Rica." Accessed Feb. 7, 2021. https://en.wikipedia.org/wiki/Costa_Rica#Religion.

———. "Partition of India." Accessed Feb. 9, 2021. https://en.wikipedia.org/wiki/Partition_of_India.

Williams, Delores S. *Sisters in the Wilderness: The Challenge of Womanist God-Talk*. Maryknoll, NY: Orbis, 2013. Kindle.

Williams, Kimberlé Crenshaw. "Mapping the Margins: Intersectionality, Identity Politics, and Violence against Women of Color." Wayback Machine. Accessed Apr. 18, 2023. https://web.archive.org/web/20230418140726/https://we.riseup.net/assets/139021/versions/1/crenshaw%20intersectionality.pdf.

www.ingramcontent.com/pod-product-compliance
Lightning Source LLC
Chambersburg PA
CBHW051929160426
43198CB00012B/2083